PACCA SERIES ON THE DOMESTIC ROOTS OF U.S.
FOREIGN POLICY

Tunnel Vision

Labor, the World Economy, and Central America

Daniel Cantor and Juliet Schor

South End Press   **Boston, Ma**

Library of Congress Cataloging-in-Publication Data

Cantor, Daniel
  Tunnel Vision
1. Central America—Foreign relations—United States.
2. United States—Foreign relations—Central America.
3. AFL-CIO.
4. United States—Foreign economic relations.
5. United States—Economic policy.
I. Schor, Juliet. II. Title.
F1436.8.U63C36 1987   327.728073   87-26406
ISBN 0-89608-333-0 (pbk.)

SOUTH END PRESS   116 St. Botolph St.   BOSTON, MA 02115

 X23

Domestic Roots Statement

Domestic Roots of U.S. Foreign Policy is a project of Policy Alternatives for the Caribbean and Central America (PACCA), an association of scholars and policymakers. Through research, analysis, policy recommendations, and the collaboration of analysts in the U.S. and the Caribbean Basin, PACCA aims to promote a humane and democratic alternative to present U.S. policies toward Central America and the Caribbean.

The principles of such an alternative are set forth in PACCA's *Changing Course: Blueprint for Peace in Central America and the Caribbean:*

> U.S. foreign policy should be based on the principles which it seeks to further in the world. These include: non-intervention, respect for self-determination, collective self-defense, peaceful settlement of disputes, respect for human rights, support for democratic development and concern for democratic values. Adherence to these principles is critical to working out practical programs for regional peace and development.

Participants in the *Domestic Roots* project endorse these principles, and seek to widen discussion of alternative policies based on them. The project explores the links between current U.S. policies in the region and major institutions and issues in U.S. domestic politics. In a series of pamphlets, *Domestic Roots* will highlight the continuity between domestic policy initiatives and current policies in the region, locate the domestic sources of current policy choices there, and assess the obstacles to and opportunities for widening debate about those policies, and constructing a decent and democratic alternative to them.

Acknowledgments

Many people helped us to write, and rewrite, this book. By now embarrassment at calling on such a large number of friends and colleagues has faded; instead we are reminded of just how deep the talent in and around the labor movement really is.

Our thanks go to Henry Abelove, Murray Auerbach, Erik Beecroft, Ron Blackwell, Sam Bowles, Lydia Bracamonte, Nathaniel Cantor, Bob Cilman, Ed Clark, Josh Cohen, Dan Dale, Colin Danby, Noel Desiderio, David Dyson, Steve Early, Margee Ensign, Gerald Epstein, Sheldon Friedman, Stan Gacek, Paul Garver, Ellen Goldensohn, Bennett Harrison, James Heideman, Alan Howard, Candace Howes, John Hudson, Todd Jailer, Nancy Jones, Maria Landolfo, Dinah Leventhal, Mark Levitan, Max Liebersohn, Roberta Lynch, Laura Markham, Robert Master, the Midwest Labor Research Center, Prasannan Parthasarathi, Cynthia Peters, Frances Piven, Sam Pizzigati, Secundino Ramirez, Joel Rogers, Lydia Sargent, DéSean Schor, Tim Sears, Robin Semur, Barbara Shailor, Janet Shenk, Dave Slaney, Fred Solowey, Bob Stark, Don Stillman, Sean Sweeney, Peter Tooker, Mark Tushnet, Winifred vanRoden, and Ken Wray.

We are especially grateful to Michael Albert, Robert Armstrong, Mary Chicoine, and Noam Chomsky.

This book is dedicated to our parents.

DC & JBS
New York City and Cambridge

I work for the union, cause she's so good to me.
J.R. Robertson
"King Harvest"

TABLE OF CONTENTS

TABLE OF CONTENT

INTRODUCTION

The Anaheim Debate

Look around the world baby,
it cannot be denied
Will somebody tell me why
are we always on the wrong side.
Steven Van Zandt
"Sun City"

Sometimes negotiations are not conclusive. Deals go sour. The would-be settlement may be down on paper, but everyone senses the disagreement percolating beneath the calm surface. On the third day of the October 1985 AFL-CIO convention in Anaheim, California, the calm was broken.

The topic was U.S. aid to the Nicaraguan contras. High-ranking staffers from the AFL-CIO's central office in Washington hoped to avoid any mention of the undeclared war against Nicaragua, reserving their condemnation for the Sandinista government. Representatives of the UAW, AFSCME, ACTWU, IUE, IAM, and other unions wanted a clear denunciation of the Reagan administration's policies of support for the contras.

Two days of backroom bargaining produced a compromise: there would be no specific mention of aid to the contras. To satisfy the conservatives, the resolution would denounce the Sandinistas; to satisfy the progressives, it would include a call for a negotiated settlement, rather than a military solution.

It was, on the whole, a soft agreement. Conservatives had held the line and prevented an explicit anti-contra position. Giving ground to progressives on general, if important, language was an acceptable price to pay for convention-floor unanimity.

1

Many individual AFL-CIO affiliates, meanwhile, interpreted the resolution as implicitly anti-contra. Contra aid, they reasoned, could never lead to a negotiated settlement. Even though an explicit anti-contra position was not adopted by the full convention, an affiliated union could take such a view without contradicting official AFL-CIO policy. Member unions—internationals, districts, or locals—had won a clear victory for their autonomy on foreign policy.

Everyone on both sides assumed that the battle was over. The resolution would pass intact, with all its gaps and contradictions barely noted.

Everyone was wrong.

Richard Kilroy, president of the BRAC (Brotherhood of Railway, Airline and Steamship Clerks), had scarcely finished reading the amended resolution to the 1000-plus delegates, alternates, and guests when the rush to the microphones began.

Kenneth Blaylock, president of the American Federation of Government Employees (AFGE), was the first delegate called on by AFL-CIO president Lane Kirkland. Blaylock was for many years a civilian employee of the Defense Department and today leads a union under severe economic pressure because of federal "reductions in force." The hall grew quiet as he spoke in the rich, rolling tones of his native North Carolina about his visit to El Salvador and Nicaragua earlier in the year.

> As I sat in a church [in El Salvador] late one night and listened to mothers...tell about the atrocities being perpetrated against them and their families by [sanitization], this technique of military operation, it would literally bring tears to your eyes.
>
> ...When we travel through those areas and we see not just homes destroyed where people maybe did support the rebel forces, but square miles and miles and miles of homes and farms destroyed, it makes you wonder what our government is all about.
>
> ...As I visited the [Nicaraguan] coffee plantations and the farms up close to the Honduran border, we talked with Miskito Indians, we talked to campesinos who do not fear the Sandinistas. They are carrying weapons from sticks to rifles to protect themselves against the contra. Then I have a young farmer tell me about an attack on his farm where his wife was raped and then killed, [and] he lost

two children, not from the Sandinistas, but from the contra.

...Now I don't know about the rest of you people here, but when I look at Iran, I look at Vietnam, I look at Nicaragua, I look at El Salvador, Guatemala, I would like for one time for my government to be on the side of the people, not on the side of rich dictators living behind high walls.

...So every fiber in my body that triggers my reflexes and my basic instincts says to me, if Ronald Reagan supports these efforts and if friends like the Coors family, who responded after Congress cut off the money to the contras...[and] started raising private funds, if these two people are for it, we damn well better be against it.

When Blaylock finished there was some tentative clapping, then more forceful applause, and finally outright cheering and whistling from a substantial minority of the delegates. For the next ninety minutes, delegates from across the country took to the mikes to denounce the Reagan administration or the Nicaraguan government.

The smoke finally cleared, and the resolution passed easily. But the routine anticlimax of the vote could not mask the significance of what had just occurred. As delegates with any memory knew, they had witnessed something momentous: the *first* floor debate on a foreign policy issue in the history of the AFL-CIO.

The debate at Anaheim surprised nearly everyone in the hall that day. Perhaps it shouldn't have, and the controversy should be seen as another symptom of the concern within the labor movement about its future. We share that concern. It has led us to write this essay for trade unionists and others who believe that a healthy labor movement is not only desirable but necessary. Our purpose is to connect the debates on Central America, AFL-CIO foreign policies, and labor's economic problems.

Our view is shaped by a reading of the last forty years of U.S. history. We believe that after the Second World War, internationally oriented banks, corporations, and government officials in the United States restructured the world economy along "free market" and "free trade" principles, and reoriented American ideology toward anticommunism. The cold war consensus was born, and it has ruled politics ever since.

Organized labor was part of that consensus. On foreign policy, labor played an important and controversial role in helping to cement the new system.

In the last fifteen years, the face of the international economic system—which we call Wall Street Internationalism—has changed. Once dominant, U.S. companies face fierce international competition. Meanwhile, money is swirling around the world with greater speed. In the modern system of production and finance, the loyalty of American multinationals and banks to the nation's welfare looks increasingly shaky.

Management has adapted, more or less successfully, to the new international game. Labor has had more difficulty coming to terms with these changes. Adherence to the cold war consensus has straitjacketed organized labor's ability to respond to problems such as the trade deficit, runaway shops, and excessive military spending.

Nevertheless, a new view is emerging. It is a reaction to the escalating war in Central America and the traumas of the international economy. It recalls the aftershock of the war in Viet Nam. Many unionists are asking whether Wall Street Internationalism and the cold war consensus really serve workers. Seeing the human costs here and around the world, they wonder what alternatives might exist.

This essay tries to articulate that view. We will discuss the reasons why so many trade unionists oppose U.S. government policies in Central America and how that opposition challenges some of the fundamentals of the AFL-CIO's worldview of the last forty years. We will show how changes in the structure of the international economy after World War II ultimately weakened labor's position vis-á-vis management. And we will conclude by arguing that a challenge to the status quo is the starting point for a strong union movement in the years to come.

Chapter One is a short description of the crisis in organized labor and the arguments being made by trade union critics of traditional AFL-CIO policy on Central America.

Chapter Two glances back at the international system constructed at the end of World War II and traces today's policies to the early postwar years.

Chapter Three discusses the incorporation of American unions into the consensus of Wall Street Internationalism and cold war thinking. The AFL, and later the AFL-CIO, came to play a role in implementing the government's foreign policy goals.

Chapter Four considers some of the economic costs of today's international system. While many American workers once benefited materially from the global system, the high price of Wall Street Internationalism, long paid by many workers and farmers abroad, is now being charged here at home.

In Chapter Five, we return to the Central America debate, where broader questions about the international system have crystallized. In our concluding chapter, we offer suggestions for a more rational, pro-worker foreign policy.

The world economy and world politics have changed since the end of the Second World War. If the labor movement is to thrive again—and that is our hope—it will have to change its view of the rest of the world, the actions it takes, and the policies it supports. We hope this essay will contribute to that urgent task.

CHAPTER ONE

Trouble in the House of Labor

Boomtown, boomtown
better be careful,
hard times in this boomtown.
Dave Alvin
"Boomtown"

The 1980s have been difficult years for American unions. Power and prestige are at their postwar low. Consider the following snapshots of working America.

° Only seventeen percent of U.S. workers now belong to labor unions, half the mid-fifties high of thirty-four percent. This percentage has been falling steadily for thirty years, but the decline has gathered steam in the last decade.

° Unions now win less than half their representation elections, and lose more than half of decertification votes. The money spent by unions on new organizing fell thirty percent from 1953 to 1974.[1]

° There have been fewer strikes in the last five years, but those who do strike are staying out longer. Management feels neither the economic pressure to resume production (due to overcapacity or out-sourcing) nor the moral and social prohibition against replacing workers with scabs (the "permanent replacements" of PATCO, Continental Airlines, Greyhound, Louisiana Pacific, or TWA).[2]

The decline of trade union power parallels a decline in the standard of living of working people.

6

° Real income has fallen by $1,300 per family since 1979, back to its 1960s level.[3]

° Unemployment, after five years of recovery, persists. Correctly measured to include discouraged workers, involuntary part-timers, and others not counted in the official statistics, the real unemployment rate is nearly fourteen percent.[4]

° Eight million jobs were created between 1979 and 1984, but sixty percent of them offered wages of $7,000 or less.[5]

° Because more women are now working outside the home, family workloads have risen. Over the last decade, the average American has lost eight hours of leisure time per week.[6]

° In a recent study of the United States, West Germany, Japan, and Sweden, our country scored lowest in both quality of life and economic performance.[7]

Real wages are down and poverty is up. It's harder to buy a home, social programs have been cut back, and the share of income and wealth going to the rich has increased dramatically. Many of these problems can be traced to the international economy.

° The 1986 trade deficit was $170 billion. The Department of Commerce estimates that the trade deficit cost the country two and a half million jobs in 1986 alone.[8]

° Large multinational banks and the International Monetary Fund have imposed a massive protectionist program on Latin America. The debtor countries are virtually forbidden to import U.S. manufactured goods or farm products. The drop in exports to Latin America accounts for more than half the decline in U.S. exports since 1981.[9]

° U.S. companies are tripping over each other to get offshore. In the last twenty years, capital flight has cost the country four million jobs.[10]

While U.S. labor has been wounded by the international economy, times have also been tough in other countries. In Europe, there are roughly twenty million unemployed people. The poor countries are in a deep depression. Hit hard by falling food and mineral prices, high interest rates, and economic slow-down, many workers and farmers have seen their real incomes halved. Hunger, poverty, disease, and social dislocation are at historic levels. Progress seems to be going in the wrong direction.

Despite all this bad news, unions are not disappearing, as some conservative *and* liberal observers would have us believe. Unions have always had to fight hard for their political and economic gains, even in the boom years before 1973. But the Reagan years have had a qualitatively different impact, and the structural damage to labor will not be easy to repair.

Today's economic questions are especially painful and perplexing because they come on the heels of the West's period of greatest prosperity. For thirty years after the Second World War, income in the United States grew about two and a half percent per year, every year. Between 1947 and 1973, the real income of the average American household doubled. (It has been dropping ever since.) This growth was due in large part to the international political and economic system set up by the United States at the end of the war. The United States assumed the stewardship of a grand, world-wide "empire," and we have just lived through its golden age.

During the golden age American workers reaped the fruits of cheap oil, affordable housing, and a revolution in consumer goods. There was little knowledge of what U.S. companies were doing around the world, and the effects of the international order on others went unnoticed. Organized labor provided support for the political, ideological, and economic presumptions of this prosperous status quo. But now, as familiar presumptions are looking unfamiliar, labor (and all citizens) must ask if the old rules still apply.

○ Are U.S. companies willing to deal with labor, or do they believe that they can and should jettison the whole collective bargaining relationship?

○ How can a labor movement confined inside national boundaries respond to multinational corporations?

These economic questions are intimately linked to political ones. The postwar international economy has been sustained by anticommunist ideology, with the world divided into two distinct spheres. That ideology in turn is the rationale for the worldwide deployment of U.S. military force and the escalation of the arms race.

The application of this policy to Central America is what has captured the attention of the labor movement. Economic uncertainty, disillusionment with our experience in Viet Nam, and a growing belief that the world is more complex than the cold war policy allows have each contributed to the questioning of once sacred truths.

Speaking Out On Central America

Whatever disagreements American unionists have about the nature of the Sandinista revolution, we do agree on one central point: the U.S. support of the counterrevolutionary forces known as the contras is illegal, immoral, and contrary to the best interests of the American and Nicaraguan people.

—American Federation of State,
County, and Municipal Employees, 1985

We call on the government of the United States to end all military support for the contras attacking Nicaragua from Honduras and Costa Rica.

—Amalgamated Clothing and
Textile Workers Union, 1985

We oppose any form of intervention in Central America, including aid to the contras in Nicaragua.

—United Steelworkers of America, 1986

Hundreds of resolutions like those above have been passed by union bodies across the country. Thousands of union members have voted to put their organizations on record against the administration's policies in Central America.

This is not entirely unprecedented. During the Vietnam War, many individual unionists actively opposed the Johnson and Nixon administrations' prosecution of the war. The Labor Assembly for Peace was formed in 1967, and many unions participated in the antiwar movement, but organized labor as a whole lagged behind the rest of society. It took thousands of American and millions of Vietnamese deaths to generate substantial labor opposition.

Labor's unwillingness to go along with a new administration's plan for Third World intervention is far more developed in 1987 than in 1967. Unions in manufacturing, the service industries, and the public sector, as well as a few in the

Opposition to Contra Aid in Organized Labor: The New Majority

The unions listed below have each taken strong anti-contra positions, either by convention resolution or executive action. Nearly all of the presidents of these unions are members of the National Labor Committee in Support of Democracy and Human Rights in El Salvador. The membership figures for all of the AFL-CIO unions are based on per capita payments by the affiliates to the central office. While membership fluctuates over time, the general point holds firm: *A majority of organized labor in the AFL-CIO opposes any and all aid to the Nicaraguan contras.*

Union	Paid Members	Fees to AFL-CIO
ACTWU	228,000	$ 754,041
AFGE	199,000	471,038
AFSCME	997,000	3,369,184
BCTWIU	115,000	382,961
CWA	524,000	1,749,305
GCIU	141,000	477,097
IAM	520,000	1,753,746
ICWU	40,000	132,584
IUE	198,000	588,571
IWA	34,000	94,249
Molders	32,000	107,688
NALC	186,000	619,107
Newspaper Guild	24,000	75,212
NUHHCE	23,000	34,800
OCAW	108,000	320,599
SEIU	688,000	2,334,573
UAW	974,000	3,248,948
UFWA (farmworkers)	12,000	40,080
UFWA (furniture)	21,000	67,552
UFCW	989,000	3,326,500
USWA	572,000	1,945,052
TOTALS	6,625,000	$ 21,892,887
As a Percent of AFL-CIO Totals	50.5%	50.3%

Anti-contra Independent Unions

NEA	1.8 million
ILWU	50,000
UE	n.a.

Related Organizations

Industrial Union Department, AFL-CIO
Coalition of Labor Union Women (CLUW)

The Other Side

AFL-CIO unions whose leaders have adopted *pro-contra* positions are the United Federation of Teachers (470,000 members), the Bricklayers (95,000), and the Seafarers (80,000).

The new anti-contra majority among AFL-CIO-affiliated unions will not translate automatically into a strong resolution at the Fall 1987 convention. The foreign policy apparatus of the federation is still firmly in the hands of hardline "cold warriors," most of them members of the rightward-leaning Social Democrats USA.

Note

The abbreviations of unions used in the table above stand for the following: AFSCME, American Federation of State, County, and Municipal Employees; BCTWIU, Bakery Confectionary, and Tobacco Workers International Union; CWA, Communications Workers of America; GCIU, Graphic Communications International Union; IAM, International Association of Machinists; ICWU, International Chemical Workers Union; IUE, International Union of Electrical Workers; IWA, International Woodworkers of America; NALC, National Association of Letter Carriers; NUHHCE, National Union of Hospital and Health Care Employees; OCAW, Oil, Chemical and Atomic Workers International Union; SEIU, Service Employees International Union; UAW, United Automobile Workers; UWFA, United Farm Workers of America; UFWA, United Furniture Workers of America; UFCW, United Food and Commercial Workers; USWA, United Steelworkers of America; NEA, National Education Association; ILWU, International Longshoremen's and Warehousemen's Union; UE, United Electrical Workers.

building trades, have adopted a stance against intervention and administration policies.

This grass roots anti-intervention sentiment in union halls across the country has been matched at the very top. National leaders of twenty AFL-CIO unions and three independent unions (including the pace-setting National Education Association) have jointly announced their opposition to all aid to the Nicaraguan contras or the Salvadoran military. As this book goes to press, fifteen national unions are campaigning on Capitol Hill and in Congressional districts for the long-overdue end to contra aid. White House efforts to keep the contras alive with sham peace plans or repackaged humanitarian aid has confused no one. Collectively, the union presidents on the anti-contra side of the fence represent more than half of the membership of the AFL-CIO (see chart above). The policies and staff of the Department of International Affairs (DIA) of the AFL-CIO do not yet reflect the diversity of opinion that exists in labor today.

Five Reasons

Why have union leaders taken the stands that they have? Why risk the displeasure of unconcerned or conservative members, or the hostility of the AFL-CIO central hierarchy?

There are five main reasons why important labor leaders and organizations have adopted an opposition stance with respect to Central America:

1. Trade unionists and their families fear that Central America will become another Viet Nam.

2. Billions of dollars of military aid are being spent in Central America, highlighting distorted spending priorities and domestic budget cuts.

3. U.S. support for anti-union governments, be they military or civilian, helps create a "better business climate" for multinational investment. But it leads to low wages overseas and runaway shops, concessions, and domestic unemployment.

4. Major backers of President Reagan's efforts to get "private" financing for the contras are prominent anti-union employers such as the Coors family, the Hunts, and J.

Peter Grace. These are unlikely allies for American labor.

5. Labor has a long tradition of international solidarity. Workers in Central America are exploited, and unions are repressed. They deserve our solidarity. And solidarity is not only morally correct, but is also American labor's best hope for confronting the globalization of industry and finance.

None of these reasons, taken separately, would have been sufficient to make a dent in the way labor thinks about foreign affairs. Taken together, they have forced many trade unionists to reevaluate the conventional wisdom.

Another Viet Nam?

West Virginia and the District of Columbia share a dubious honor: they lost young men in Viet Nam at the highest per capita rate in the nation.

They share a second, and happier, distinction: a work force that is among the most unionized in the country.

On reflection, this is not really a coincidence. The armed forces have always been able to depend on the coal mining and chemical industry families of West Virginia and their counterparts in the black working-class neighborhoods of the District. Needless to say, Washington's contribution to the war in Viet Nam did not include the sons of congressmen.* (Only one son served.) As a rule, Congress is much better at sending other people's children off to die. This memory of Viet Nam helps us understand the most profound source of labor opposition to intervention.

---

* The aptly named chicken hawks in Congress, think-tanks, and the administration (Elliot Abrams, Sen. Paul Trible, Rep. Newt Gingrich, Pat Buchanan, Robert Leiken, and company) who are leading the propaganda barrage against Nicaragua are a clever bunch, but no amount of cleverness can mask the fact that they all worked hard (and successfully) to avoid being drafted during the Vietnam war. It makes their special efforts to send young Nicaraguans, contra or Sandinista, to their deaths, all the more hypocritical.

President Reagan and the so-called neo-conservatives have tried to wipe out that memory. There have been countless articles by conservative intellectuals on the Vietnam syndrome, by which they mean the unwillingness of Congress and the American people to blindly support U.S. military actions around the globe. The Republican leadership, their Democratic soul mates (Nunn, Robb, Bradley, etc.), and the neo-cons have largely succeeded with Congress and the media.

In the labor movement, they have not been quite as successful: the price paid by, and the lies told to, the families of those who actually fought and died in Viet Nam have not been so quickly forgotten. Even though U.S. ground troops have not been introduced into Nicaragua (they are already on the ground in El Salvador, Honduras and Panama), there is widespread labor skepticism toward Reagan's account of the "threat" to U.S. security. Support for Washington's version of foreign affairs is no longer automatic. Contragate has only reinforced the belief that the State Department will lie to (or "disinform") the public when required. For Reagan, Bush, Abrams, North, Secord, and the rest, the lesson of Viet Nam was not that we should be reluctant to play world policeman, but that we should keep the press and public in the dark, and pay other people to do the fighting.

Of course, Nicaragua is not Viet Nam. Nicaragua is smaller, poorer and weaker. There are less than three and a half million people in Nicaragua. (The population of Viet Nam is more than fifty million.) The administration may be able to minimize the loss of U.S. lives in Central America by a combination of the low-intensity contra war, aid to the Salvadoran and Honduran armies, and U.S. tactical support. It is a cynical strategy, but perhaps the only feasible one, given the level of public hostility to intervention. Despite arduous efforts to manage the news from Central America, too much contrary information seeps through. Many Central America correspondents are avoiding the Vietnam era mistake of relying primarily on official sources. An SEIU local leader put it well: "There's just too many reporters down there who can talk Spanish with the people and find out what is really happening."

As Vietnam veterans and their antiwar contemporaries rise through labor's ranks, the State Department has more and more trouble defining the issues and disguising the true costs of intervention.

Misuse of Public Money

The United States is now spending almost ten billion dollars a year on military and security operations in Central America, as Josh Cohen and Joel Rogers point out in an earlier contribution to the PACCA Domestic Roots series, *Inequity and Intervention*. This money is part of a fantastic rise in the total military budget, which has transformed the mix of public expenditures. Ten billion dollars—whether for U.S. bases in Honduras (the S.S. Honduras, as one reporter called it), or aid to the contras—is, of course, small potatoes compared to Star Wars. But unionists who have seen civilian jobs and services gutted recognize the connection. Cuts in the domestic budget that compensate for high military expenses are having a direct and indirect impact on the lives of the working and middle classes. The direct effect is clear: cutbacks in job training and employment, the privatization of public services, and reduced health and childcare programs. States, counties, and municipalities are suffering from reductions in revenue sharing, block grants, and housing subsidies. The indirect impact is felt in the shrinking social wage—cuts in unemployment insurance or food stamps—that make it harder for workers to take on management for fear of losing a job, even an unpleasant one. Union power is weakened as the holes in the safety net get bigger.

Defense spending is a holy sacrament under Reagan; tampering with it a mortal sin. The response of many unionists is best symbolized by a popular button among delegates to a 1986 communications workers' convention: "Money for school lunches, not for contras."

The Regional Sweatshop

Job losses at home connect with repression abroad. The U.S. government pressures poor countries to provide a "better business climate," a familiar code word for cheap wages and weak (or non-existent) unions. The Commerce Department is sponsoring a program to attract U.S. industries to the fifty-cents-per-hour border towns with Mexico, against strong AFL-CIO opposition.

The business climate throughout Central America and the Caribbean is of this better variety. Despite the slick brochures produced by the American Chamber of Commerce in Guatemala, Jamaica, or El Salvador, the transfer of these industries does not lead to prosperity. Wages are held down by alliances between

Wages and Competition:
A Race to the Bottom

A basic prinicple of unionism is to "take wages out of competition," in order to prevent employers and governments from using one group of workers to undercut a second. In our era, it has been irresistibly easy for corporations to travel around the globe in search of cheap wages. The chart below suggests why Central America and the Carribean are a choice locale for earning superprofits.

The numbers also make clear the economic interest of U.S. workers; without powerful unions overseas to limit corporate greed, competing on the world market means little more than a race to the bottom.

Company	Weekly Wages	Benefits
Levi-Strauss (El Salvador)	$20-22	$4
Levi-Strauss (Ark./Tx.)	$240-285	$50-60
Munsingwear (El Salvador)	$15	$3
Munsingwear (Ala./Minn.)	$250-$300	$50-60
Johnson & Johnson (Grenada)	$30	$6.60
Johnson & Johnson (N.J./Ill.)	$540	$100-$150
MacGregor Sporting (Haiti)	$24	$2.40
MacGregor Sporting (Wisc.)	$275	$60
Ky. Fried Chicken (Guatemala)	$9-15	n.a.
Ky. Fried Chicken (Calif.)	$135-200	n.a.
Castle & Cooke (Honduras)	$30	n.a.
Castle & Cooke (Calif.)	$400	$60
Chrysler (Mexico)	$63	n.a.
Chrysler (Michigan)	$537	n.a.
Zenith (Mexico)	$35	n.a.
Zenith (Illinois)	$316	$138

Sources: Union Research Departments and U.S. International Trade Commission.

curity forces and anti-union business interests, and average
ss than $30 per week. Any honest account of industrialization
d foreign investment in Central America must recognize the
ccompanying social dislocation, slums, and damage to the
gricultural sector. Despite billions of investment dollars by mul-
nationals, banks, and the U.S. government, the standard of
ving throughout the Caribbean basin (which includes Central
merica) is declining.

trange Bedfellows

Labor is also hostile toward White House actions in Central
merica because of the involvement of the American Right in the
nancing of the contra war. Unavoidably, contra supporters land
 bed alongside the most right wing, anti-union elements in our
ciety. The Iran-contra hearings have revealed how sordid per-
nal gain was as much a motive of these ex-soldiers and
ndraisers as their supposed commitment to democracy.

Of course, profiteering disguised as patriotism is nothing
w. Neither is the lunatic Right, which will still be with us long
ter the contra war runs out of steam. What is startling is the
spectability the contras and their U.S. promoters receive in
nservative business and social circles.

The Coors Brewing Corporation is, as usual, second to none
 its dedication to the contras. The only other cause the Coors
others have shown similar enthusiasm for is breaking the
ion at their brewery in Golden, Colorado. This landed them on
e AFL-CIO boycott list in 1978 and kept them there for almost
n years.

Coors is not alone in combining an anti-union creed at home
ith support for reactionaries abroad. Indeed, the American
ight has never lacked consistency in this regard; Henry Ford's
tred of the UAW and admiration for Nazi Germany comes to
ind.[11]

Understandably, the right wing's contra-fever colors the issue
r many trade unionists. While guilt by association can mislead,
e Coors connection gives pause to many a union member and
ader.

lidarity Knows No Borders

The U.S. labor movement has a strong tradition of interna-
nal solidarity. For many years U.S. workers have supported

the battles of foreign workers—financially, morally, and politica
ly. Solidarity in Poland, Coca-Cola workers in Guatemala, ar
South African miners are prominent examples. Aid can be coo
dinated by the AFL-CIO (Solidarity); it can be given through t
International Trade Secretariats that link similar unions fro
different countries (Coca-Cola); or it can be union-to-union (t
United Mine Workers involvement with their South Afric
counterparts).

These battles for justice—against a Soviet-dominat
regime, an American multinational, or a racist government—a
more similar than they appear at first glance. To workers on t
receiving end, oppression is oppression. American unionists w
give aid to, or get help from, workers elsewhere are participati
in one of the noblest traditions of the labor movement.

Within labor, there is a growing awareness that internatio
al solidarity has practical, economic meaning. Low wages
Central America and the Caribbean can't help but drive dov
wages in the U.S. For refugees fleeing violence in Centr
America, often the only option is to come to the States, whe
they frequently work as undocumented workers. Los Angeles
now the second-largest Salvadoran city in the world. Latin-sty
inequality is being re-created inside our borders (or just outsi
them, as in the industry along the Texas-Mexico border). T
precarious status of undocumented workers makes them ripe f
sweatshop exploitation.

The worldwide search for low wages and high profits—t
globalization of manufacturing and finance—has not be
matched by a similar globalization of labor. Labor is at a treme
dous disadvantage in international battles. The barriers of la
guage, culture, and politics hamper cross-national organizing
workers. Labor's resources are meager in comparison
management's, and international coordination is expensi
Unions in different countries making common cause against
multinational corporation is rare, with progress at 3M, Gene
Motors, or Unilever more the exception than the rule. It will ta
time to build a labor culture that can challenge the well-defin
global business culture. (The Trade Secretariats are therefc
very important, as they are the logical sites for such efforts.)

Trade unionists are finding that their problems can no long
be solved solely in a national context. Genuine internatior
solidarity among unions is crucial in the fight against multir
tional power, anti-union governments, or runaway shops.

The Stecel 10

A dramatic example of North American solidarity with embattled workers in Central America was the campaign to win the 1984 release of the so-called STECEL 10. Imprisoned without charge or trial for four years following an unsuccessful strike, these Salvadoran power plant workers were finally freed by President Duarte after pressure from U.S. trade unionists. The public relations cost of keeping them in jail had become too high, despite the insistence of the U.S. Embassy that the original strike was political, thereby nullifying any claims of labor rights violations. But many U.S. unions felt that the violation of human and trade union rights overwhelmed the hesitation that the embassy and some labor conservatives felt at working for the release of the leadership of a center-left union.

The dispute over the jailed Salvadorans symbolizes the contradiction at the heart of much of official AFL-CIO policy in Central America: the all-or-nothing, for-us or against-us standard by which unions in other countries are measured was not up to the task of understanding the meaning of the STECEL brothers' imprisonment.

The leadership of that union is and was left of center; some may support the rebels fighting against the government and the army. This should not come as a complete surprise, given that the army and its associated "private" security forces had massacred more than twenty workers and family members before, during, and even after the strike, going so far as to arrest, torture, and murder the wife and daughter of the union president, Hector Recinos.

The union is an important representative of working-class discontent and aspirations. To deny it recognition can only harden anti-American feeling in the plants, ports, and farms it represents. Labeling a union Marxist-Leninist achieves two ends: it stifles debate inside the U.S. labor movement, and in the Salvadoran context it opens up the union so-named to governmental or quasi-governmental terror.

strengthens unions overseas and, in turn, shores up labor's position here at home.

Solidarity—North and South

In Central America, international solidarity is especialltricky because workers there are entangled in the cold war Union federations that are colored "red" by the Department o International Affairs of the AFL-CIO, and there are some in eacl country, are not eligible for support.

Nevertheless, more and more Americans understand that the life-and-death problems of workers in Central America shoulc not be lost in the drama of superpower politics. People have heard of death squads in El Salvador and Guatemala and knov that their targets are often trade union leaders and members Common decency has moved many trade unionists unfamilia with the intricacies of Central American politics to raise thei voices against this brutality.

Certain Central American unions may well be "political" o "leftist," two common charges made by the Department of Inter national Affairs. Under the same circumstances U.S. unionist might well want to raise political or leftist demands such as th dismantling of death squads or an end to austerity.

In the pages that follow, we examine the political attitude that guide the Department of International Affairs of the AFL CIO, and try to determine—by reviewing the origins of labor' postwar foreign policy—why simple acts of internationa solidarity have become so complicated.

CHAPTER TWO

The Creation of
Wall Street Internationalism

> *I'm so glad I'm*
> *living in the U.S.A.*
> *Yes I'm so glad I'm*
> *living in the U.S.A.*
> *Anything you want we got it*
> *right here in the U.S.A.*
>> Chuck Berry
>> "Living in the U.S.A."

Origins of the Postwar Economic System

The attitude of the AFL-CIO's Department of International Affairs towards the Central American conflict can be traced to the international economic and political relations established in the closing years of the Second World War. That is where we begin our story.

For America, as for many countries, World War II changed everything—politics and culture, housing patterns and race relations, and of course, the economic system. The early postwar period saw the revamping of the international economic order. By economic system or economic order, we mean the principles, laws, institutions, and understandings by which international business is conducted.

The economic system that emerged at the end of the war has been called by various names—Bretton Woods, *Pax Americana*, or the open world economy. We call it *Wall Street Inte* *nationalism*, because it combined internationalism (the promi of an open world economy) with Wall Street (the interests large, East Coast-dominated multinational corporations ar banks).* The principles trumpeted by economic conservativ today are those on which the international system was buil First was "free trade." Second was "free mobility of capital." Ar third was "free exchange of foreign currencies." The rules of Wa Street Internationalism were:

1) Few or no restrictions (such as tariffs or import quotas) on trade between nations.

2) Free movement of capital investment and profits from one country to another.

3) No limitations on the buying and selling of foreign currencies.

The effect of these free market principles** was that no country had the right to enact regulations that might insulate it from powerful outsiders. Disturbances caused by the global economy would have to be endured, on the yellow brick road to a better future. Poor countries would have to open themselves to foreign capital and guarantee its safety. Rich nations would have to allow imports from each other. These rules of the game were enshrined in brand-new institutions of global reach—the International Monetary Fund, the World Bank, and the General Agreement on Tariffs and Trade (the GATT).

But Wall Street Internationalism, or WSI for short, was much more than these principles and institutions. It was also the codification of U.S. economic and political power. WSI was

---

* We do not mean to imply by this designation that the U.S government was uninterested in the new system. The government especially the State Department, played a leading role in designing and implementing the postwar economic arrangements.
**We use the term free market with caution. There have never been (and probably never will be) markets which resemble the textbook ideal. The supposedly voluntary nature of markets can only exist i participants in the market are of equal power. In the real world where unequal power is the rule, market exchanges will alway involve coercion of one sort or another.

designed in part to guarantee the global dominance of large American corporations and banks.

The connection between U.S. power and a free market system was straightforward. In the game of world market, a "free" market (i.e., WSI) allows the strongest players to win, because the rules prevent the weak from "protecting" themselves. American corporations were by far the strongest in the world at the time the game was set up, and America was the most powerful nation. The U.S. acted just as the British had in the nineteenth century: the strong preached free trade to the weak.

The system that emerged from the war was clearly Made in America.[1] As conceived by the government and internationally oriented banks and corporations, WSI held out the promise of new markets, cheap imports, and access to natural resources. Among businesses, many large companies had developed a strong international orientation during the 1920s and 1930s. Prominent examples were General Electric, International Harvester, and the Ford Motor Company.[2] These soon-to-be highly multinationalized companies pushed hard for free trade. The leading international and investment banks, particularly the Morgan and Rockefeller interests, were also pro-WSI. Among the media, the *New York Times* was chief advocate of the new order. And as we shall see, organized labor was partially incorporated into the pro-WSI alliance.

The oil industry had its own special interest: to take Middle East oil out of British control. The U.S. companies succeeded: their share of Mideast oil, virtually zero before the war, rose to nearly sixty percent by the early 1950s.[3]

The economists, bankers, industrialists, and politicians who designed WSI were responding to the two central economic events of their lifetimes: the Depression of the 1930s and the wartime boom that followed. The combination of these two events was powerful and led them to a preoccupation with the question of markets.

The basic problem during the lean years of the thirties had been the failure of purchasing power to keep pace with the economy's ability to produce. As productivity soared during the preceding decade, there was not enough demand to match the supply of goods. The repression of unions in the 1920s by both employers and government had kept wages down, but the side effect was equally low levels of consumption. The working class

How WSI Solves
Trade Deficits with Unemployment

The free market principles of WSI spell bad news for workers in countries with trade deficits (such as the U.S. has today). Under WSI a trade deficit is almost always eliminated by raising unemployment.

Perhaps the most common factor causing a trade deficit is a rapidly growing economy. With rapid growth, corporations import more raw materials and consumers buy more foreign goods. Unless trading partners are expanding at comparable rates, exports are unlikely to increase in tandem.

One way for the government to deal with the trade deficit would be to put on import controls, but that violates WSI. Instead the government will probably raise interest rates, run a recession, and generate unemployment. This will reduce imports and lure investors looking for a high interest rate.

This scenario isn't inevitable. An alternate plan designed by the British economist John Maynard Keynes was nixed by U.S. bankers and conservative politicians. If his plan had been adopted, American workers would be facing a more pleasant future. Keynes' main concern was jobs, and in his plan every country could pursue policies which would lead to full employment. He figured out early on that the proponents of WSI were constructing a global economy which would prevent precisely that.

Imagine that there are only two countries in the world. If one country (the U.S.) is importing more than it's exporting, the second country (say Japan) must be exporting more than it's importing. Now who should adjust? The deficit country or the surplus country?

The U.S. is importing heavily because it's growing rapidly. In order to reduce its trade deficit, it must scale back on imports by reducing its economic growth. This lowers imports from Japan and causes unemployment there also. Why not let Japan adjust by growing faster and importing more? This raises U.S. exports and solves its trade deficit. If the surplus country (Japan) adjusts, there's less unemployment in both countries. If the deficit country (the U.S.) adjusts, there's more unemployment in both.

The Keynes plan said the surplus countries should adjust. But this was a novel idea which violated the longstanding opposition of financial interests and other conservative businessmen to rapid growth. They feared the inflation and growing strength of labor that often accompanied fast growth. So it was never adopted. Instead, under WSI, deficit countries must do the adjusting. The protests of U.S. officials that Japan and West Germany (the big surplus countries) should grow faster illustrate the point. The system was designed to prevent exactly that!

was weak. The industrial organizing of the 1930s increased workers' purchasing power and evened the score somewhat, but these early battles were as much for union recognition and survival as for higher wages. Surplus capacity and slack demand remained the dominant feature of the decade.

The war changed all this. The federal government became a guaranteed consumer, and the economy boomed. Firms added to their productive capacity at an unprecedented rate. In 1946, the economy was capable of producing fifty percent more than six years earlier.[4]

At war's end, an obvious and terrifying question emerged: Who was going to buy the goods that the government had purchased during the war? When factories reconverted to civilian production, how would the nation's increased productivity be absorbed? Was another depression inevitable?

The solution favored by most of the business community was to export to foreign markets. The increased capacity of our factories could be absorbed overseas. But there were major obstacles to U.S. exports. One was protectionism. Another was the power of European business monopolies. A third was the entrenched colonial empires of the European powers, particularly Britain.

In addition to restricting access to the markets of their own countries, the European powers had erected sturdy tariff walls and imperial preferences throughout their colonies. Eliminating imperial preference—the special trade terms with the colonies—had been high on the agenda of American business and government for a long time. In the postwar period, U.S. economic and military power was finally sufficient to make it happen.[5] An WSI was the form it took.

The Cold War, Anticommunism, and Wall Street Internationalism

It would be a mistake to conclude that the proponents of WS won an easy victory. They did not.

Many European capitalists opposed the new system, but the could not match the Americans. The war's destruction and th need for U.S. aid convinced them to accept the sometimes quit generous terms offered. Washington demanded free trad pledges as a condition for participation in the Marshall Plan, th massive foreign aid project begun in 1948 that rebuilt Europ while stimulating demand for American exports. Agreeing to th American conditions was not too high a price for the battere leaders of European finance and industry.

It should come as no surprise that European workers ha even less ability to dictate the terms of their postwar status. Th European labor and resistance movements opposed, albeit un successfully, what they perceived as U.S. domination of the domestic economies. They were wary of leaving econom recovery to random corporate investment. Some Europea unionists preferred a higher degree of government interventio and regulation in the style of the British economist, Joh Maynard Keynes. Others supported still more radical proposa for workers' councils, participation on corporate boards, socia ized industry, and grass roots democracy. WSI had little popula support.

In the United States, WSI faced a mixed bag of opponents. included domestically oriented companies, many Midwest-base and hostile to the East Coast financial interests who advocate the new order. American followers of Keynes, often tied to th labor movement, preferred a more managed system on th grounds that it would make full employment easier to achiev Finally, the Eightieth Congress of the United States (1947-49 which had to approve the institutional elements of WSI and th Marshall Plan, was controlled by conservative Republicans isolationist bent.

With such a broad coalition arrayed against them, how we the supporters of WSI able to win?

Whether the fight was against Congress on the issue of aid to Europe, or against European unions on the future of their countries, the proponents of WSI eventually discovered a sure-fire tactic for disarming their opponents: the Soviet threat. Anticommunism combined a deep-seated fear of the Soviet Union with that of radicals here at home.

In early 1947, President Truman incorrectly characterized the Greek civil war as a struggle between democracy and totalitarianism, and the leading Senate Republican on foreign policy, Sen. Arthur Vandenberg, advised the President on how to get his program through Congress: "scare hell out of the American people." In the event, Congress approved aid to Greek "freedom-fighters." The combatants on one side were drawn largely from the anti-Nazi resistance. On the other side were the former Nazi collaborators and their allies. The United States ended up supporting the latter.

In 1948, foreign policy planners began to talk about containing the Soviet Union. By 1950, the newly formed National Security Council called for a rollback of Soviet influence throughout the world (including the Soviet Bloc) by the expansion of U.S. military might.

As it turned out, military power did not roll back the Soviet Union, but it was crucial to the victory of WSI. The U.S. had the nuclear monopoly and was not hesitant to remind others of it.[6] Instead of disarming, as many had hoped and Congress had mandated, the Truman administration embarked on a military build-up. Military spending exploded, from $13 billion in 1950 to $50 billion in 1953, with only a fraction directed to the war in Korea. This rearmament program marked the beginning of a continuing military presence around the globe. And it gave birth to a network of military-related corporations dedicated to the permanent production of war materials—what President Eisenhower named the military-industrial-complex.

The American government built bases in forty countries around the world—more than 350 by the 1980s—and took on the role of world policeman. Between 1946 and 1975, U.S. overseas forces were deployed for political purposes an average of once every seven weeks, excluding the wars in Korea and Indochina.[7] Today nearly half the Pentagon's 300-plus billion dollar budget supports this capacity for intervention in the Third World.

Meanwhile, Republican reactionaries raised the banner of anticommunism here at home. An obscure Congressman from

California, Richard Nixon, catapulted into national prominence by his investigation of a communist connection in the back ground of an up-and-coming diplomat, Alger Hiss. In Hollywood a B-movie actor whose career was in decline, Ronald Reagan, became head of the Screen Actors Guild on a promise to purge communists from the movie business. In 1950, Senator Joseph Mc Carthy of Wisconsin denounced communist influence in the State Department and later in the army.

For those of us who did not live through these years, it is almost impossible to imagine the intensity of anticommunism in daily life. Across the country, police departments formed Red Squads to keep track of suspected subversives. Production workers, government employees, and teachers associated with communist or radical causes lost their jobs. In some communities, right wing groups visited local drug stores to make sure that paperbacks by authors such as Hemingway, Faulkner, and James T. Farrell were not being sold.

By the early 1950s, most people had accepted anticommunism, the cold war and the principles of WSI. Doubts about the new arrangements were overshadowed by economic prosperity. An explosion of consumer goods and services put what had once been luxuries within reach of most working families: new homes, new cars, washing machines, college for the kids. The American dream seemed to be a reality.

It is not our intention to suggest that the origins of anti-Sovietism can be credited solely to the planners of WSI. The Soviet Union was hardly an innocent bystander, as rising tensions and mutual suspicions in U.S.-U.S.S.R. relations generated self-fulfilling prophecies about each superpower's behavior. Our central point is that the cold war and WSI converged neatly. Anti-Sovietism, as the historical record reveals, was consciously used to achieve the economic and political objectives of American policymakers and corporate leaders. Notwithstanding the realities of Soviet rule, cold war ideology was used to justify WSI and the dominance of U.S. corporations and the government around the world.

The brilliance of those who orchestrated the system was that they equated their objectives with the ideals of democracy and freedom. This was no simple task. To a great extent, WSI eroded the conditions of life for workers and farmers around the world. In Europe and Japan, living standards rose but political dissidents were stifled. In the poor countries, hunger and poverty in-

The Cheap Banana

The new system promised cheap raw materials, which became a cornerstone of postwar prosperity. Whether it was bananas from Central America, oil from the Middle East, rubber from Southeast Asia, sugar, rice, textiles, silver, zinc, or aluminum, poor countries didn't get much for their exports. If and when they did, companies in the rich countries raised the prices of what the poor countries imported.

One barometer of the grip of WSI is the value of the "primary" commodities, minerals and agricultural products exported by the poor countries, relative to the prices of manufactured goods they import from the rich countries.

This measure, excluding oil, fell throughout the 1950s and 1960s. By 1972 it stood at only two-thirds of where it had been when WSI began. The same was true of oil prices. A barrel of Saudi Arabian crude fell from $ 1.75 to 72 cents, accounting for inflation. The formation of OPEC in 1973 was, in retrospect, the logical harvest of the oil companies' exploitation.

For U.S. workers, the "benefit" from low raw materials prices is easy to identify but hard to calculate. With cheap imports, American workers were able to buy more. Purchasing power and the standard of living rose.

Whatever the gains to American workers, the real winners were multinational corporations. A company manufacturing shirts in Hong Kong or importing bananas from Guatemala will charge as much for its goods as the market will permit. The losers were the many workers and farmers in the poor countries whose standard of living deteriorated. Despite repeated attempts to raise the prices of commodity exports, the "terms of trade" for poor countries continue to worsen.

Mainstream economists and their corporate sponsors offer eloquent defenses of the virtues of "free trade" and cheap imports. Consumers gain, developing nations develop, and everyone wins. History suggests otherwise, and reveals that the greatest victories are always won by the merchants and manufacturers who do the trading.

creased. For them, the claim that the system operated in th
name of the extension of democracy rang hollow. Nonetheles
the cold war enlisted the support of many Americans precise
because they were convinced it was the way to promote freedo
not because they wanted to protect the profits of Chase Manha
tan or General Electric. The self-interest of American busine
was cloaked in the rhetoric of idealism and democracy, a
American workers were, in a sense, victims of a gigantic co
fidence game.

In the end, the victory of WSI was not total. While its adv
cates successfully installed market principles around the wor
they could not immediately or completely eliminate the barrie
they opposed. Many of the provisions took years to implement.

Limitations on European currency trading were n
eliminated until 1958. The International Trade Organizatio
which was supposed to bring down tariffs and end quotas, nev
got beyond the planning stage. In its place the less-ambitio
GATT was set up. The European Common Market turned out
be a managed, not an open system. In the poor countries, t
International Monetary Fund and U.S. corporations have oft
been frustrated in their attempt to install free market principl
Nevertheless, America's, or at least Wall Street's vision carri
the day. Free market internationalism became the offic
doctrine of international economic relations. The world econo
moved in a free market direction and U.S. corporations co
solidated their position.

The Domestic Scene and the Social Accord

While the organizers of WSI were battling for their fr
market philosophy in the Congress and overseas, they also h
to reckon with the American trade union movement. Th
needed cooperation, and worried about getting it.

Labor had come of age. Both federations, the AFL and t
CIO, had prospered during the war. In 1946, the AFL had so
7.8 million members, and the CIO (only ten years old) had gro
exponentially to a membership of 4 million. The CIO set the p
with victories in auto, steel, rubber, and other mass producti
industries, but the AFL had by no means abandoned the field
its younger rival. A notation in the journal of a CIO organizer

est Virginia tells the story of the pace of organization in those ears: "I organized nine locals today..."

When the war ended, American unions used their new rength in the greatest strike wave in U.S. history. This was a fferent kind of strike. Labor was now a legitimate and spected social institution and a valued partner in the emocratic Party. The life-and-death struggles of the thirties ere over. The fight for recognition from both management and ociety had been won. Unions turned their attention to achieving ie economic gains postponed by the austerity of the war years.

But labor was in for some hard times. Before playing ball ith unions, business and government wanted to cut them down size. The we're-all-in-this-together attitude of the war years anished and was replaced by corporate America's determination ot to lose further ground. It was not simply a question of money. he issue was control. From the companies' point of view, the rosion of management rights and the readiness of the American orker to disrupt production with wildcat strikes had to end. hese were serious roadblocks to the efficient exploitation of the pportunities so clearly in view in the world economy.

Perhaps labor overrated its strength. The AFL and the CIO, till separate federations, competed fiercely. Longstanding politi-al differences continued to flare up in individual unions. In 1946 peration Dixie, an ambitious plan to organize the South, ogged down in internal conflict over race relations, manage-ent opposition, and compromises within the Democratic Party ot to challenge the power of white southern Democrats.

In 1947, Congress joined the fight on management's side by assing the Taft-Hartley Act. Labor's strongest weapons—the econdary boycott and the sitdown strike—were abolished. State egislatures won the right to abolish the union shop with the so-alled right to work prohibition. And in a sign of the times, union fficers were required to swear that they were not members of he Communist Party before the union could use the procedures f the National Labor Relations Board. Taft-Hartley reduced abor's power and paved the way for what historians call the ostwar social accord.

This social accord was the domestic side of WSI. It was not a act or contract in any formal sense, although the UAW-GM con-ract of 1950 was close to a written form of it. It was an under-tanding between labor and management about what each could expect of the other, and it set the terms of industrial relations fo thirty years.

For workers, the accord promised predictable gains in wage and benefits. The economy hummed along and blue-colla workers shared in its riches. For management, the accor guaranteed the right to make all decisions on production, prii ing, and investment. For union officials, three-year contracts o fered stability in a potentially unstable climate. Wildcat strike tapered off, and labor-management relations were routinized an institutionalized.

The labor movement was not unanimous in its support fo the social accord and Wall Street Internationalism, or for tha matter, integration into the Democratic Party. The late 1940 were marked by an internal battle within the CIO over just thes questions. Beneath the surface, a careful listener could hear th early rumblings of McCarthyism. Spurred on by Congress an business (both eager to weaken labor), this internal battle preoc cupied the union movement, and the momentum of the war year disintegrated.

The result was the expulsion, in 1949 and 1950, of eleve: unions whose Communist or leftist leaders refused to sign loyal ty oaths. Despite the high organizational price, in both number and morale, the pro-expulsion forces were determined to ous their leftist rivals. It was not an era when the right to unpopula political opinions carried much weight. For the left, the expul sions violated the fundamental principle of solidarity, a solidarit more necessary than ever given management's new attacks.

In hindsight, it is clear that the lack of unity and the gradua dissolution of labor's left wing made it easier, not harder, to at tack unions. Removing the radicals did not convince employers politicians, and the media to stop their assault. It whetted thei appetite.

The left-led unions had provided much of the energy and so cial vision of the labor movement. The blurring of that broade vision, even at its most naive or utopian, marks a crucial transi tion in American labor history. It has meant less organizing o the unorganized, less mobilizing of the membership, and les stomach for tough political fights.

Even so, unions did not surrender in the 1950s and 1960s They fought hard on the shop floor and politically, protecting the interests of their members. But labor was unwilling or unable to

obilize for a deeper restructuring of power. A booming economy
d the ideological grip of the cold war discouraged boat-rocking.

By the 1970s, major reform movements—women's rights, the
tiwar movement, and environmentalism—enjoyed important
pport from some unions, but labor as a whole was an inconsis-
nt ally. Complacency set in, bureaucracy grew, and important
ctions of organized labor lost the aggressive edge that had so
orried corporate America.

What did the social accord yield for American workers?
here is no simple answer, and one must be careful to specify
hich workers and when. For the one-third of the workforce that
as organized, the accord—built on the base of Wall Street Inter-
tionalism—brought prosperity. U.S. domination of the world
arketplace rebounded to the advantage of business, workers,
d unions. There was no real competition in any important sec-
r. Raw materials were cheap, U.S. products were in great
mand everywhere. Boosted by exports, government spending,
d a climate of optimism, the economy grew rapidly. The "pie"
as expanding, and there seemed little reason to doubt the per-
anence of an affluent America.

To Blacks, the accord delivered less, although substantial
umbers made gains as union members in basic industry.
omen, pushed out of high-paying jobs after the war, were of-
red bit parts in the accord through their husbands. For the un-
ganized, who remained the great majority of workers, the
uits of the accord spilled over, but erratically and partially.

Organized labor's gains in the postwar years were impres-
ve, but the price was increasing isolation from other progres-
ve causes and the sacrifice of a broader social and economic
genda. Instead, labor accepted the role of junior partner in a
anagement-government-labor alliance in support of Wall Street
ternationalism and the cold war. As we shall discuss in chapter
ve, this unequal partnership would prove painful later on.

By the 1984 Presidential election, the weakness of organized
bor's strategy was apparent, as Republicans and many
emocrats engaged in orgies of union-bashing unimaginable two
ecades earlier. Business had become the general interest, and
bor was relegated to the special category. That the business
mmunity's claim is fraudulent is beside the point. Corporate
merica has a comprehensive vision, if a self-serving one. Labor
oes not.

CHAPTER THREE

From Marseilles to Managua: Labor's Role in the Creation of WS

Money changes everything.
Tom Gray, for Cyndi Lauper,
"Money Changes Everything"

The AFL in Europe

As it turned out, labor supported both the social accord an the system of Wall Street Internationalism. This suppor whatever the economic gains to working-class Americans, wou not have been possible without anticommunism. Labor got di tracted. In the new political climate economic justice at hom took second place to fighting the cold war.

The central event of the time was the Marshall Plan, which the political desire to fight the Soviets meshed with tl humanitarian desire to aid Europe. The Marshall Plan promise to satisfy both desires, with benefits on both sides of the Atlanti

The enormous sums of money for rebuilding Westen Europe's factories, roads, and cities would return as purchases American goods. Demand and domestic employment would sta high. It was Keynesianism at its most compelling.

The economic aid would have political effects as well, boos ing U.S. prestige and goodwill among European workers. reconstructed Europe would mean reconstructed unions, an American policymakers were keen to influence the politic character of those unions.

Many communists had emerged from the war as popular union leaders because of their resistance to fascism. Some were politically subservient to Moscow, but they were also militant unionists who fought hard to protect jobs and wages. The architects of WSI needed a more pliable working class and considered these unions too unreliable.

In the United States, working-class support for the plan was solid: it was the obvious way to help West European society, industry, and unions. Although some CIO unions criticized the Marshall Plan as a way for American business to re-create Western Europe in its own image, most were supportive. One-half of the CIO's membership was of Eastern European origin, themselves immigrants or the children of immigrants. The sounds of Soviet domination of their mother countries reverberated through the homes of the American working class in a very personal way. Letters from relatives arrived, describing the economic suffering and political deep-freeze of life in Eastern Europe during Stalin's last years. Anticommunism was on understandably fertile ground.

American policymakers needed help in advancing the WSI cause within the European labor movement. They looked to the AFL, where support for the Marshall Plan and the cold war flowed easily and naturally. To an important degree, its leaders shared the perspectives and goals of business and government leaders.

Thus, the worldview of labor's postwar foreign policy had its birthplace on the ports and in the factories of France, Italy, Germany, and Greece, the new battlefields of Europe. The shooting war was over, and the battle now was for the hearts, minds, and loyalties of European workers. On one side stood conservative and Christian Democratic unions; on the other, radicals, socialists, and communists.

As early as 1944 the AFL worked with the U.S. government to provide economic resources and political support to conservative unions in Europe. Money and advice were given to bolster unions deemed "democratic" or, if not democratic, at least sympathetic to American interests. Funds came from a combination of government, corporate, and union sources.

In France, as George Meany explained, the AFL financed a split in the communist-led union, chose the leaders of the breakaway group, and ultimately helped produce a dual (later, three-sided) labor movement that is easily the weakest and most

The Port of Marseilles

In 1949, in the Mediterranean port of Marseilles, France a communist-led longshoremens' union went on strike against a shipment of Marshall Plan supplies. The strike was undermined by AFL and U.S. government funding of Italian strikebreakers. The CIA's Thomas Braden, who authorized the government payments, reminisced about the effort in a magazine article twenty years later. The AFL needed money, he wrote,

> ...to pay off strongarm squads in Mediterranean ports, so that American supplies could be unloaded against the opposition of communist dockworkers...When they ran out of money they appealed to the CIA. Thus begin the secret subsidy of free trade unions...Without that subsidy postwar history might have gone very differently.

Braden and others have repeatedly justified such intervention as necessary to block communist influence. A compelling case can certainly be made that the French dockworkers' union was manipulative and cynical. But the AFL's program of fighting back with undemocratic and secretive tactics of its own, allegedly on behalf of democracy, strikes a false note. Breaking the strike and the union helped in the construction of a friendly France, but it did not help the workers, communist or not. The Marseilles dock episode is but a prominent example of this contradiction in the AFL's overseas organizing.

Source: Thomas W. Braden, "I'm Glad the CIA Is Immoral," *The Saturday Evening Post*, May 20, 1967.

inept in Western Europe today. In Italy, they helped the anticommunist and Christian Democratic unions fight the more militant communist and socialist groups, coordinating their efforts closely with the State Department. Money for this project was solicited from U.S. corporations with investments in Italy, on the theory that they had an interest in less aggressive unions.

In Germany, the AFL's European representatives actually selected the leaders and organizations that would receive preferential treatment from the Allied military authorities, with scarcely a nod to the wishes of German workers. The favored German unionists were judged not on their record of fighting fascism, but on their attitudes towards the U.S.S.R. As the recent trial of Klaus Barbie revealed, U.S. government officials recruited Nazis in their efforts to influence the course of postwar Germany. And in Greece, the AFL abandoned its distaste for state-sponsored unions and worked closely with government-appointed labor officials in an attempt to consolidate anticommunist influence inside Greek unions. The unfortunate but unsurprising result was a weakened workers' movement, left and right.*

In each case, the money, advice, and direction was given secretly. Why? Was the enthusiasm of European workers for American-style unions not quite as high as after-the-fact justifications claimed? Was there something undemocratic in the AFL's reluctance to let Western Europe's workers decide for themselves? Was the AFL's characterization of Continental politics as a battle between democracy and totalitarianism an accurate one?

These questions point to a flaw in the decision-making of the U.S. unionists. The notion that a few American officials in what was then called the Free Trade Union Committee could judge what was best for the workers of another country violates democratic principles. It is contrary to our own labor history. All too often, the Lovestone-Brown conception of democracy meant denying European workers the kinds of organizations they wanted in favor of a more corporate-dominated unionism. (Jay

---

* Readers interested in a solid introduction to AFL activities are encouraged to read Chapter 20 in Jonathan Kwitny's excellent book, *Endless Enemies: The Making of an Unfriendly World*, (New York: Congdon and Weed), 1984. Another useful source, if somewhat heavy-handed, is Ronald Radosh's *American Labor and United States Foreign Policy*, (New York: Random House), 1969. A personal and engaging account is also contained in Victor Reuther's *The Brothers Reuther and the Story of the UAW: A Memoir*, (Boston: Houghton Mifflin), 1976.

Lovestone, the head of the Free Trade Union Committee, wrot
the blueprint for the AFL's foreign operations. This dedicate
and intelligent ex-communist rarely missed an opportunity to d
battle with his former allies. Irving Brown was Lovestone's ke
European representative. Before the war, Brown had bee
prominent on the conservative (and losing) side in the UAW'
struggle to get organized. His distaste for progressive unionist
in the UAW was apparently transferred intact to Europe. Brow
retired in 1986, and was replaced as DIA director by Thoma
Kahn, who retains his predecessors' anticommunist fervor.)

Most European unionists share our commitment to politica
democracy and civil rights. Many also hold a deep devotion t
socialism or economic democracy, which frightens corporate an
governmental elites who see such ideas as threats to privileg
Lovestone, Brown, and other American labor representative
who joined in that assessment did no service to their Europea
friends

In 1949, the International Confederation of Free Trad
Unions (ICFTU) was established in London, with the support
the AFL, the CIO, and the British Trades Union Congress.* Th
new confederation was the industrialized West's response to th
Moscow-dominated World Federation of Trade Unions (WFTU
The AFL and the dominant CIO faction considered the WFT
less a confederation of unions than a political arm of the Sovi
Union.

Eventually, the labor situation in Europe began to resemb
that of the United States. For the most part, the left wing union
were defeated, and their vision of a better world obscured.
loose network of anticommunist unions had been create
European labor's options were circumscribed by the cold wa
and workers' demands for radical change had been cooled b
postwar prosperity.

---

* Before the 1955 merger of the AFL and CIO, both federations ha
European offices and staffs. The AFL's was larger and more close
linked to the U.S. government—financially, and politically. Fe
serious scholars deny the ties between the AFL's European operati
and the American intelligence agencies. The CIO retained a mo
independent, worker-oriented approach to foreign policy, which w
gradually lost after the merger. See Kwitny.

From Europe to Latin America

The AFL's main efforts were in Europe, but the rest of the world was not ignored. Latin America, located within the United States' traditional sphere of interest, was a favored arena for labor activity.

An AFL office for the region was established in 1946, headed by a colorful ex-spy named Serafino Romualdi. It evolved into the regional branch of the ICFTU. Known by its Spanish initials, ORIT, it became the principal vehicle for U.S. labor influence in Central America and the Caribbean during the 1950s.

The most dramatic involvement of American labor "south of the border" before 1960 is worth re-telling. Despite the passage of some thirty years, it remains a relevant and depressingly familiar story.

The Fatal Weakness

It is 1954 in Guatemala. The elected government of Jacobo Arbenz challenges the status quo of a plantation economy and powerful military. Early success in land reform and the expansion of union organizing provoke a counterattack camouflaged as a fight against communism and for democracy. Arbenz is a populist, not a communist, but his land reform program so unnerves the powers-that-be, especially the U.S. banana companies, that the CIA engineers a *coup d'etat*.

What of labor's role? In 1953, before the coup, Romualdi and ORIT unsuccessfully attempt to build a conservative dual union. Just ten days after the army takeover in 1954, they are back in Guatemala advising the new dictator, Armas, on labor policy. Armas, writes Romualdi, "himself favors the development of free trade unionism."[1]

AFL President Meany has similar feelings. "The American Federation of Labor," he states, "rejoices over the downfall of the Communist-controlled regime in Guatemala, brought about by the refusal of the Army to serve any longer a Government that had betrayed the democratic aspirations of the people and had transformed the country into a beachhead of Soviet Russia in the Western Hemisphere."[2]

Like Humphrey Bogart in *Casablanca,* Meany was "misinformed." Guatemala in 1954 was not a matter of communism versus democracy, the U.S.S.R. against the U.S. It was about overturning a feudal social system. It was about challenging a

powerful U.S. company (United Fruit) and its Guatemalan allies
on issues of land reform, union recognition, and living standards.

Some American unionists recognized this at the time, and
spoke out. Emil Mazey, secretary-treasurer of the UAW (CIO)
charged that

> ...we have been supporting the wrong people...the State
> Department and the United Fruit Company have been
> manipulating the politics of that country. They have or-
> ganized revolutions in the past against the best interests
> of the people. They have opposed land reform. They have
> opposed any special progress for the people of Guatemala
> and then we wonder why the communists who make
> promises of land reform, who make promises of social
> security and other necessary gains for the people, wind
> up on top. I say we have to change this foreign policy of
> ours. We have got to stop measuring our foreign policy on
> what's good for American business that has money in-
> vested in South America and elsewhere in the world.*

Unfortunately, Mazey's was a minority voice. The louder
voices portrayed Arbenz' challenge to inequality and exploitation
as an assault on U.S. security and values. The result was dis-
aster.

The "democracy" that the coup brought about was a fiction,
and union leaders and members paid a heavy price in the new
Guatemala. Since then, the military regimes that followed Arbenz for thirty-two years have murdered more than 100,000
people. Political leaders, trade unionists, and poor peasants have
been dragged from their homes and shot in the street. In 1983
alone, human rights groups estimate that 10,000 civilians were
killed by the military in a plan to eradicate radical opposition
and guerrilla insurgency. Genocide is not too strong a word to
use in describing the Guatemalan government's treatment of its
own people. Today there is a saying in that country that if you
want to visit a union leader, go to a graveyard.

---

* Mazey's speech was echoed thirty years later in the UAW's 1983
  Executive Board resolution about another Central American conflict:
  "We must abandon our embrace of the country's [El Salvador's]
  oppressive elite and place the U.S. back on the side of democratic
  change where we rightfully belong."

The AFL's mistake in Guatemala was not only backing the
ong people, but thinking about the situation incorrectly. It is
sy to see the 1985 Anaheim debate prefigured in the conflict
er the Guatemalan coup. The debacle that resulted from U.S.
:ions there is sad verification of a comment made by the UAW's
.lter Reuther in another context:

> The chief weakness of American foreign policy is the
> predilection of our State Department for dealing with
> anybody who will promise to hate Communism. It is fatal
> to resist Communism by courting reaction.[3]

As it turned out, hardly anyone learned much from these
ents. Guatemalan history has repeated itself many times since
54, only never as farce. It has stayed a tragedy.

The Birth of AIFLD

It took the 1959 revolution in Cuba for Latin America to
.erge center stage in U.S. foreign policy. Castro's victory
.nned American policy makers. The shock waves reverberated
ough the AFL-CIO's Department of International Affairs.

The labor response to events in Cuba was the creation of the
nerican Institute for Free Labor Development (AIFLD,
.nounced A-Field). AIFLD's stated purpose was (and is) to
vide training, assistance, and money to trade unionists in
.ntral America, South America, and the Caribbean. Few ac-
ities of the AFL-CIO have been so controversial.

As in Europe, the motivating force was anticommunism.
.ce again, an alliance was created among American labor, busi-
ss, and government. And once again, a training program was
.ked to an aid program, the Alliance for Progress.

AIFLD opened its doors in 1962 with a blue-ribbon Board of
rectors. Besides top labor leaders, it originally included busi-
ss executives from corporations with investments in Latin
nerica, among them the Rockefeller interests, W. R. Grace Co.,
.ited Fruit, St. Joe's Minerals, and Pan American Airlines.[4]

All believed that a series of Cuban-style revolutions would
vitably occur if poverty and deprivation were not alleviated.
.e rich Latin oligarchies were digging their own graves and
.esented an obstacle to multinational investment. A new for-
.la that blended social progress, economic growth, and political

pluralism would effectively fight populist movements ar weaken the oligarchs. AIFLD's goal was to create conditions f economic growth in an atmosphere of political stability. Physic brutality and economic exploitation of farmers or the urba working classes needed to be reduced. Repression and violen against workers, the thinking went, earned short term profits the expense of long term prospects. Radical movements wou flourish under such conditions.

Economic growth would reduce the pressure at lower leve of society, and "free trade unions" could represent the interests those who, until now, had only the radicals to champion the cause. The AIFLD-assisted unions would be an attractive alte native to the leftist unions while simultaneously fighting t right wing landowners and businessmen who resisted any cha ges in their privileged status. These unions would not threate basic privileges and would be a bulwark—in a favored phrase "against extremists of both the left and right."

Controversy followed AIFLD from the beginning. In Braz President João Goulart attempted to regulate foreign oil inte ests and carry out a land reform. He was denounced as a cor munist and his government eventually collapsed under rig wing pressure in April 1964. Three months later, AIFLD lead William Doherty boasted in a radio interview that AIFL trained workers had been directly involved in "the clandesti operations" of the overthrow.[5] A succession of military office followed Goulart, and the labor movement languished und police repression for the next twenty years.

In 1963, the elected President of Guyana, Cheddi Jagan, w overthrown in another coup. He charged AIFLD involvement his ouster, and documents released later backed him up. Fro 1962-1965 in the Dominican Republic, AIFLD-sponsored du unions joined the business and military campaign against Pre dent Juan Bosch's reforms. A U.S.-supported military coup fin ly toppled the Bosch government. Post-coup investments Dominican resorts by top U.S. labor leaders further damag American labor's reputation in that country.[6]

Controversy about AIFLD has never ceased. It dies down f a time, only to flare up again whenever a Latin governme pushes for major reforms. Just prior to the bloody 1973 Chile coup d'etat that brought down President Salvador Allend AIFLD training dramatically increased. During the cou

AIFLD-supported unions helped the military conspirators by keeping communications and port facilities open.

The current controversy is in El Salvador. In 1985, an AIFLD-sponsored federation publicly challenged the government of Salvadoran President Napoleon Duarte to deliver on its promises of land reform and peace. It was an embarrassing demand to the Duarte regime and AIFLD, as this federation was the base of Duarte's 1984 election victory. AIFLD's response was to set up yet another new federation, charging that its earlier creation had been co-opted and infiltrated by guerrilla sympathizers. It seems that any demands of Latin workers which coincide with those of revolutionary movements are, for AIFLD, proof positive of their illegitimacy.

Thinking About AIFLD

There are two evaluations, one positive and one critical, of the theory and practice of the AIFLD project.*

The positive view is that, by and large, AIFLD has succeeded in its efforts to build up centrist, democratic unions. Their unions have won some economic gains, provided political calm in tumultuous circumstances, and resisted the destabilizing demands of the radical unions. They have blocked communist expansion and simultaneously advanced social reform. The battle (against the left) continues on a daily basis, but generally the anticommunist unions have succeeded in providing an outlet for the aspirations of working people and their families.

The battle (against the right) for land reform and higher wages has produced mixed results, and must go further. Any

---

* American labor's influence in the Caribbean basin nations is immeasurably larger than in South America, due to size and geography. The nations of Central America and the Caribbean are smaller and closer, and are consequently the preferred target for direct military intervention. There have been thirty-odd U.S. military interventions in Central America and the Caribbean since 1900, whereas the *first* introduction of U.S. troops into the continent of South America was the 1986 Bolivian drug raid. The distinction between Central and South America is an important one, especially to Latin Americans themselves.

Funding AIFLD

That AIFLD and the State Department rarely disagree should not be too surprising, given their financial relationship. Nearly all of the work that AIFLD does in Central America, the Caribbean, or South America is funded by the federal government. The dependence on federal dollars was high from the start, but has reached overwhelming proportions under Reagan. In AIFLD's early years, the $15 million it cumulatively received from the U.S. government represented between sixty percent (1962) and ninety-two percent (1967) of its total budget.

By 1985, the $19.4 million yearly budget was nearly ninety-eight percent federal money, with less than two percent from the dues payments of union members.

Is the government "buying" cooperation? Not necessarily. Financial ties notwithstanding, AIFLD sometimes departs from a State Department line. But on the whole labor's international affairs leadership and the policymakers at the State Department look at the world in the same way and come to the same conclusions. State Department money simply makes life easier and projects bigger. In 1985 the AFL-CIO spent $39 million on domestic affairs. The foreign affairs budget was $41 million. It would take the doubling of per capita payments of the ninety-three affiliate unions to allow the federation to continue its projects without government funding.

defects on this score are attributed to the obstinance, stupidity or arrogance of right wing business forces, not to any faults i the AIFLD-sponsored unions themselves.

Overall, the positive analysis credits the centrist unions Central America and the Caribbean with the important virtue having endured. Caught between rightist intransigence and lef ist manipulation, this is considered a substantial victory.

The more critical account acknowledges the value of some AIFLD's secondary work, such as housing or agricultur cooperatives. Its failures, however, outweigh these modest gain This view rejects AIFLD's preoccupation with the communi

AFL-CIO BUDGET 1985

**Domestic
$39 Million**

**Overseas
$41 Million**

Departments

Organizing
Information
Economic Research
Education
Legislative
Legal
Civil Rights
Community Services
Occupational Safety,
Health and Soc. Sec.
Political Education

**Headquarters
Administration**

**Regional Office
Operations**

(Atlanta, Fort Worth,
NY, SF, Chi., Tulsa,
Balt., Boston)

**Headquarters
Non-Administrative**

(Labor Institute on
Public Affairs,
Meany Center,
Building Expenses,
Contributions, etc.)

Latin America

Africa

Asia

Europe

Dept. of Intl. Affairs

Income from Membership Dues: $50.1 Million
Income from Federal Grants: $37.6 Million

threat: the main problem in the hemisphere is not Soviet, or
Cuban agitation, but a legacy of unjust and brutal exploitation.
The centrist unions are stronger on paper than in reality. They
are no more democratic than their rivals—unless democracy is
simplistically equated with the use of pro-American rhetoric. In
some cases these unions were established in an attempt to oppose and weaken existing leftist federations. Unfortunately, the
weakening of the radical* unions is usually followed by a resur-
gence of power among the oligarchy and the multinationals. Corporations and powerful landowners prefer moderate unions to
radical ones. Mostly, however, they prefer no unions at all.

A Third World nation anxious to capture a share of foreign
investment knows that its main selling point—sometimes its
only one—is low-wage labor. A reputation for restless workers or
labor militancy is a black mark, and politicians, bankers,
manufacturers, and military elites will resist earning one. In
such situations, AIFLD unions often prefer not to rock the boat.
For example, many of the AIFLD groups in Central America are
associations of small farmers with little relevance to traditional
unionism. They don't bargain collectively and do not figure in the
calculation of an investor looking for a docile labor force. And its
urban federations rarely challenge military governments on
human rights issues, or adopt tough collective bargaining stan-
ces.

The obsession—and it is nothing less than that—of AIFLD's
leadership with fighting radical unions detracts from the real
battle in Latin America and the Caribbean—the battle for a
higher standard of living and for recognition that the laboring
classes are entitled to full participation in society's decision-
making. AIFLD's Doherty gave a crisp version of the narrow cold
war worldview in a 1966 speech, and there is little evidence that
much has changed in this section of the labor movement during
the last twenty years.

---

* Unions are radical, in this view, because the situation demands
  radical response, not because one country is exporting revolution to
  another. Trade unionists may recognize the exporting revolution
  claim as a variation on the third-party-interference or outsider
  theme they've heard from management and union-busting
  consultants during organizing drives.

The key question of our times is the future road of [Latin America's] revolution: toward communist totalitarianism or toward democracy. For the American labor movement this is one of the paramount, pivotal issues; all other questions...must remain secondary.[7]

It is dangerous, and sad, when such opinions become the policy of our labor movement, because they do not reflect a particularly pro-labor point of view. More often than not, fighting communism in Latin America has meant fighting worker and peasant rights.*

Finally, we believe that the willingness of corporate executives to cooperate with AIFLD is not a reflection of their desire to replicate our system of domestic labor relations in foreign lands. It is a desire to avoid it at all costs.

The contradiction of working with an administration or with corporations of dubious pro-union sentiment was remarked upon many times during the Anaheim debate. The UAW's Victor Reuther once described the trouble with the AIFLD model this way:

In the long history of the American trade union movement, no legitimate official would ever have considered giving U.S. corporations a joint role in training union members for union leadership posts...In this case, the notion that Latin American workers—so often exploited by Standard Oil, Anaconda, Grace Lines and other corporations—would have allowed the multinationals to subsidize the training of their union leaders boggles the imagination.[8]

---

* Ironically, AIFLD at times has chosen to support communist-led unions. In Brazil today, the genuinely progressive federation, the CUT, is politically independent of both Washington and Moscow. It does not fit neatly into cold war slots, and challenges management and the state in a truly radical manner. AIFLD supports its rival, the pro-Soviet CGT, because it is relatively tame and does not seriously question the power of political or economic elites. The independent CUT, like COSATU in South Africa, refuses to participate with the AFL-CIO Institute in its region.

Assessing the Past

For more than forty years, union leaders—George Mean first among equals—have accepted the argument that the expan sion of Wall Street Internationalism would benefit worke: around the world as it had benefited their own members. Today disillusionment with certain parts of the system—especially fre trade—has not yet dissuaded Meany's successors of their bas loyalties.

It is testament to the lasting genius of the architects of WS and the cold war that they were able to merge the genuine democratic values of average Americans with the self-interest multinational corporations and banks. American capital su ceeded abroad by reducing freedom to the free market. The tru meaning of democracy—popular control—was transformed int support for Wall Street Internationalism and the cold war. I reality, it has meant less democracy (especially in the Thir World) and more opportunities for multinational corporatior and Pentagon planners to exercise their talents.

Finally, there is labor's own inability to escape the logic the cold war and the accompanying obsession with anticom munism. The AFL-CIO Department of International Affairs see the world only in the black and white of East versus West. Ther are no shades of gray, and the ideological battle between freedor and totalitarianism is fought and re-fought every day. It is th smoke from these battles that the DIA uses to obscure what : really happening in Central America, in the Philippines, or i South Africa.

The DIA is stuck in the 1950s. Either you are pro-capitali: or pro-communist, pro-American or pro-Soviet. There is no nor alignment, no third way, no alternative model of economic an social development.

CHAPTER FOUR

Wall Street Internationalism Hits Home

*They're closing down the textile mill
across the railroad tracks
Foreman says these jobs are going boys
and they ain't coming back to your
hometown.*

Bruce Springsteen
"My Hometown"

In the preceding chapter we criticized much of labor's foreign policy. The cold war straitjacket has put us on the wrong side of political struggles. Over the years when workers reaped economic benefits from the international system, troubling questions about the costs of progress went unasked. But times are changing. WSI is now proving to be a very expensive proposition for U.S. workers, between the nastiness of the international free market—job loss, wage competition, and declining social spending—and the tax burden of the "empire's" military force.

A far-sighted observer in 1947 might have anticipated the runaway shop, wage concessions, and the military burden. But these predictable consequences have been worsened by a development few could have foreseen: the rapid decline of U.S. power. Almost as soon as the system got going, the American position began to slip. The American century lasted twenty years.[1] The United States now finds itself in economic competition with Japan, Europe, and even some poor countries of the Third World.

Corporations have attempted to place the burden of this com
petition on their workers. While executives have gotten record
salaries, insider stock tips, and golden parachutes, workers have
been treated to wage reductions, layoffs, and decertification
drives. Despite concessions to save jobs, businesses have brough
in foreign goods under their own name, or moved their plant
overseas. The true colors of the American multinational ar
beginning to show through, and they are not red, white, an
blue. The only color in evidence is green.

The decline of U.S. power is leading to a growing divergenc
of interest between workers and their employers. Many com
panies are becoming more and more internationalized—after al
that's what WSI was about in the first place. Government an
business elites are abandoning many industries. Not coinciden
tally, they are often those with unions.

As we look back, the irony is obvious. The labor movemen
helped to create Wall Street Internationalism. Now that syster
is doing it in. Labor stayed national, while capital went interna
tional.

In this chapter, we describe the enormous economic change
of the last forty years. Our story has three parts—competitio
from Western Europe and Japan, changes in North-South rela
tions, and the ups and downs of the dollar. We will see how thes
developments have affected working people and argue that th
price labor is paying has been high. Maybe too high.

International Competition and How U.S. Firms Ran Away From It

The new international system promised open access t
markets and the unrestricted flow of capital throughout th
world. At first, these arrangements greatly benefited U.S. co
porations, banks, and workers. Many markets were open t
American-made goods. The U.S. invested capital around th
world and could often dictate the terms.

By the early 1970s, many of these advantages had becom
disadvantages for American workers. For starters, an open tra
ing system was exposing U.S. companies to stiff competitio
most of it from Western Europe and the Pacific. Of course, th
competition was to be expected. WSI allowed for transfers
technology and capital, and the war-gutted economies of Wester

U.S. Falters as Multinationals Hold Steady

Share of World's Manufactures

	1957	1966	1977	1983
U.S.	21.3	17.5	13.3	13.9
U.S. multinationals	17.5	17.6	17.7	n.a.
U.S. multinationals' foreign operations	5.8	8.2	9.7	10.0

Source: R. Lipsey and I. Kravis, "The Competitiveness and Comparative Advantage of U.S. Multinationals, 1957-1983," Working Paper #2051, National Bureau of Economic Research, October 1986. 1957 figures are not strictly comparable.

Europe and Japan were the beneficiaries. With postwar reconstruction, they got the advantages of modernized factories, U.S. capital, and the latest technologies.

But these countries continued to gain ground long after the initial catch-up. The U.S. share of world exports fell continuously through the 1950s and 1960s by about one-third. Japan and West Germany doubled their shares, and the European Common Market increased its share fifty percent. The poor countries of the world joined the U.S. on the losing end, with a decrease of almost one-third.[2]

Why could the United States not keep up? A common view is that U.S. companies can't compete, that they have grown fat and lazy, that management puts too much emphasis on short-term profits. But a careful look at the evidence yields a different conclusion, one that suggests workers are suffering far more from competition than business.

To understand what has really been happening, we need to distinguish the United States as a nation from U.S. multinational companies. Statistics like these on shares of world exports tell us about the United States as a country and how it fared relative to other countries. They measure how products made in this country performed in the international marketplace. But they miss how U.S. multinational corporations are doing in their production outside the United States. A Ford factory in Brazil shows up in Brazil's share, not the U.S.'s. This difference is crucial to understanding today's debates on trade.

Multinationals as a whole have not suffered the loss of competitiveness that the United States as a country has. If we include the foreign operations of U.S.-based multinational manufacturing corporations, we get a very different picture of the trade situation. Overseas operations have been *gaining*, not losing in the competitive struggle. The overall share of U.S. manufacturing multinationals, which includes both their domestic and overseas operations, has held steady for thirty years. At the same time the United States as a country was losing its share. In other words, U.S. corporations are doing very well in their operations in other parts of the world, but not in their exports from the United States itself.

To a large extent, the much-decried decline of American industry is due to a long-term refusal by companies to modernize and invest domestically. Manufacturing corporations are abandoning their domestic workforces because they are abandoning the United States as a production location. The results have shown up as "captive imports," runaway shops, and out-sourcing.*

Companies are going abroad for one simple reason: they think they can make more money there. We can see it in the numbers: the percentage of total corporate profits generated abroad has risen steadily during the postwar period.**

While many corporations have held their own by going abroad, workers have not. Our ballpark estimate is that since 1966 capital flight has cost slightly over four million manufacturing jobs, or more than 200,000 per year.[3] The largest numbers of jobs were lost in machinery, such as construction equipment and machine tools, steel, automobiles, paper, printing, and agricultural products.

---

* Captive imports are goods imported by U.S. companies and sold here under an American brand name.

**WSI also encouraged overseas investment by keeping the value of the dollar high. This made it cheaper for U.S. companies to build plants overseas and more expensive for them to export from here. See the section on the dollar below for more on this.

Overseas Investment

U.S. businesses have overseas assets worth $760 billion, and a total of six and a half million employees. Since the Second World War overseas investment has expanded sixteen-fold. By contrast, U.S. GNP grew half as much. The book value of foreign direct investment grew about ten percent per year.

About seventy percent of this investment and four and a half million of the employees are in Europe, Canada, and Japan. While overseas investment is often associated with low cost labor, the bulk of it has always gone to the high wage countries with large markets.

Investment in the poor countries is about thirty percent of the total, with two million employees. Historically, most of this investment has been in natural resources, a large portion of it in mining and oil production. There has also been a search for low-cost labor, especially in industries such as electronics, footwear, textiles, and apparel.

Sources: Data on size and location from "U.S. Direct Investment abroad: Operations of U.S. Parent Companies and their Foreign Affiliates," U.S. Department of Commerce. Growth of investment from A. MacEwan, "Bankers, Slackers, and Marketeers," Working Paper, University of Massachusetts at Boston, 1982.

Overseas investment also reduces workers' income compared to corporate income. Using the most recent estimate of this loss, we have calculated what capital flight is currently costing workers. In 1986, the average U.S. worker lost $900 in income, compared to what he or she would have earned if there been had there been no capital flight.[4] Labor's income is lower because there is more unemployment, and less machinery in the workplace, which lowers productivity.

The pain of this corporate strategy can be found across the country: in the devastated steel towns from Pennsylvania's Monongahela Valley to Birmingham, Alabama; in abandoned electronics operations from New York to California; in clothing and textile shops from Massachusetts to the Carolinas; and throughout the rust belt of the Midwest.

Responding to the Competition

While there is growing attention to foreign competition, it is fair to say that the U.S. has not had a sustained or concerted national response. One reason is now obvious: our large and politically powerful multinational corporations find themselves on both sides of both oceans. Imports are not all foreign anymore; "our" companies own them. A second reason concerns the large banks, who have traditionally encouraged a high value for the dollar. Expensive dollars make for expensive exports, which discourages domestic production.

In the late 1970s the Carter administration did try to improve America's ability to compete in the world market. The value of the dollar was continually lowered, which boosted U.S. exports and discouraged imports. For a time, Carter's dollar devaluation worked—in the sense that the U.S. trade share stopped falling. But eventually it led to inflation, and Carter was forced to abandon it.

The Reagan administration's economic policies have *reduced* competitiveness. The dollar has been kept high, notwithstanding its fall in 1986 and 1987. Due to a sluggish economy, productivity has not increased much. In contrast to the opportunities for speculation, mergers, and overseas investment, there have been few incentives for productive investment domestically.

The only export the administration has promoted is military hardware—to the tune of $30-35 billion a year. Major customers include Israel, Egypt, Saudi Arabia, and Pakistan.

True to form, the administration has brought the Cold War into the Trade War. Some of the political conflicts of the Reagan period, particularly within NATO, are over economic issues. For example, Reagan attempted to block the Soviet-European gas pipeline—a $25 billion project that provides substantial benefits to European business. Perhaps the administration resents the geographic and political edge of Europe in East-West trade.[5] This U.S.-European competition may even be exacerbating the cold war itself, as the U.S. government uses anti-Sovietism to maneuver Western Europe squarely back into the American camp.[6]

Poor Countries and the Global Expense Account

As the rich countries were fighting it out, the poor ones tried to take advantage of opportunities within the system of Wall Street Internationalism and the post-Vietnam crisis of U.S. political and military power. They pursued an agenda of independence, which included a rise in oil and other commodity prices, the expropriation of U.S. overseas assets, continuing movements for political independence, and competition in the production of manufactured goods.

These developments provoked a concerted response from business and government. Commodity prices are down and political independence movements are increasingly met with military force. Taxpayers and social service recipients are footing the bills for the military's spending spree. There's an important lesson to be learned here. Maintaining an "empire" is expensive, especially during periods of resistance.

In the early 1970s, commodity prices reversed two decades of decline, and rose to all-time highs. Non-oil prices increased nearly fifty percent. And of course the price of oil soared—from $1.30 to $9.76 a barrel in real terms. The result was a historically unique transfer of wealth from North to South.*

In their indomitable style, corporations tried to shift the burden of the price hikes onto U.S. workers. Rather than borrow the money back from the OPEC producers, in order to keep up investment and maintain employment, the rich countries went into a deep recession. Unemployment rose, and corporations tried to reduce wages. Ultimately, they were successful, and workers' incomes suffered.

Business faced a second form of resistance. Governments in poor countries began expropriating U.S. foreign assets. For two decades after the end of World War II, almost no one dared threaten U.S. capital. Assets around the globe were safe and sound, backed up by U.S. military and political power. From 1946-66 expropriations occurred at a rate of less than one company per year.

---

* Of course, within the South the effects were uneven: oil-importing countries suffered, while oil-exporting countries benefited. Within the benefiting countries, the upper classes gained relative to the poor.

After 1966 things changed. There were seventy-nine takeovers from 1966 to 1971, and fifty-seven in 1972 and 1973.[7]

Historically, American property overseas had been protected by "the threat of...economic sanctions and the U.S. capacity for local military intervention, either overt or covert."[8] What had changed was the ability of the United States to take military action, and the reason was Viet Nam. As long as the country was mired down in war, intervention elsewhere was almost unthinkable. Expropriation was safer for host governments.

Viet Nam was also a symbolic boost for another kind of resistance—political independence movements. Since Viet Nam, the Portuguese have been defeated in Angola and Mozambique, and dictators overthrown in Iran, Nicaragua, Haiti, and the Philippines.

In recent years, some poor countries have begun to challenge the U.S. in manufacturing. The vast majority of manufactured goods consumed in the North are still from other Northern countries. But in the last ten to fifteen years—aided by the International Monetary Fund and World Bank programs to promote exports—newly industrializing countries have successfully begun to export manufactures. Exports from Asia have been growing at slightly more than five percent per year; the figure for Korea is about fifteen percent.[9] Companies from some poor countries are joining the ranks of the Europeans and the Japanese as competitors to American corporations.

Squeezing the Poor Countries

During the Reagan years, the agenda of the low-income countries has been drastically curbed. In 1980, triggered by the tight money policies of the Federal Reserve Board and a rise in oil prices, the world economy nose-dived into recession. This caused a sharp fall in the prices of the exports of the poor countries. Even though the world economy began to expand after 1982, commodity prices have continued to fall, with many reaching their lowest level in four decades. And the price of oil collapsed, from a $26 high to a $9 per barrel low.

Since they have the highest proportion of commodity exports, the lowest income countries have been particularly hard hit. Income in many African countries has actually been falling; poverty and starvation result. At the same time, the rich countries raised trade barriers against the poor countries, making it harler for them to export. These barriers are twice as high as those that the rich countries erect among themselves.[10]

Meanwhile, for countries indebted to banks, the Reagan years have been a nightmare. There is now more than $1 trillion of debt outstanding. The origin of this debt was the oil price hike of 1973 and the recession that followed. When the rich countries didn't borrow petrodollars to expand production, the banks lent it to the poor ones.

The combination of world recession, falling commodity prices, and high interest rates made repayment impossible, particularly for the Latin Americans nations who owe about half the debt. By 1982 *real* interest rates on the debt rose to over twenty percent for some Latin countries.[11]

The banks turned to the International Monetary Fund (IMF) as their bill collector, and it has obliged the financiers, taking the heat off private interests. Under the IMF programs, debtor countries are forced to export aggressively. Then they must hand over their export earnings to the banks. Debtor countries are now net capital exporters to the creditor countries.

In Latin America, the IMF has demanded increases in food prices and cuts in wages and government subsidies. The result has been increased malnutrition and starvation, and even economic difficulties here in the United States. Aggressive food exporting from these countries has driven down world food prices, and aggravated the farm crisis here.

The banks' demands create a huge protectionist wall around Latin America. Normally, a large percentage of the export earnings of Latin American countries would go to purchase U.S. goods. But now the banks are pocketing those earnings. Of the drop in U.S. exports from 1981-85, nearly ninety percent can be attributed to the drop from Southern countries and fifty-five percent from Latin America alone.[12] The solutions to the debt crisis now on the horizon involve a taxpayer bailout of the international banks. Having bled Latin America dry, the banks are looking to middle America.

The hardship for the poor countries is profound. The adverse combination of falling export prices, rising interest rates, and world recession has diminished their Gross National Product by nearly eight percent.[13] For comparison, the severe recessions of 1973-75 and 1980-82 reduced U.S. GNP by about two percent.

On the political front, poor countries have been subjected to greater intrusions of U.S. political and military power. And of course, there is the militarization of Central America, which we take up in the next chapter.

Those who have suffered most are the workers and peasants of the poor countries. But the squeeze on poor countries has been no bargain for U.S. workers either. The worldwide recession which drove down commodity prices left millions of U.S. workers unemployed and underemployed. It devastated whole communities. The bankers' solution to the debt crisis is squeezing the farm sector and eliminating millions of export-related jobs. To top it off, we are paying huge sums of money to maintain the armed forces. Military operations in the Third World alone cost the average American family about $1400 per year.[14] That's pretty expensive for a peacetime military.

U.S. Workers and the Value of the Dollar

WSI has taken the U.S. dollar on a roller coaster ride. Most Americans know that millions of jobs have been lost on account of the rise in the dollar since 1981. What is less familiar is why the dollar rose, why it is consistently too high, and how only a change in the rules of WSI will solve the dollar problem. In a nutshell, the problem is that the dollar is not only the U.S. currency, but also serves as world money. That means there are lots of people around the world who have a stake in a high dollar. In fact, WSI is biased toward a high or *overvalued* dollar, which hurts U.S. workers because it makes it hard to export. Today the dollar's role as world money is an albatross around our collective neck.

It should be no surprise that the monetary rules of WSI established after World War II held special benefits for the United States. Most important was the decision that established the dollar as a substitute for gold. The dollar was literally as good as gold. The U.S. Treasury promised to redeem gold for dollars at a fixed price.* This meant the United States owned the printing press for the world's money.

---

* This provision was a concession to the bankers who wanted a gold standard in order to restrict the amount of credit in the system.

The Value of the Dollar

What is the value of a dollar? How can money have a price? In international economics, the value of the dollar is just its price in terms of the currencies (or monies) of other countries. So the U.S. dollar has a price in terms of British pounds, Japanese yen, or Mexican pesos. It's the number of pounds, yen, or pesos which trade for each U.S. dollar, and it's called the exchange rate, or the value of the dollar. These exchange rates are set by trading in foreign exchange markets. Frequently, the value of the dollar is calculated in terms of a group, or "market basket" of foreign currencies.

What determines the value of a dollar? Like many other things, we can think of the value of the dollar as being determined by supply and demand. Whatever increases the demand for dollars raises their value. Whatever increases the supply of them, lowers it.

Consider imports. When American consumers want to import cars from Japan, we have to send our dollars to Japan (supply dollars) to trade them for yen, which is what we use to buy cars with. Of course, the consumer doesn't actually send the dollars abroad, but some U.S. importer has to. So imports cause dollars to be "supplied" and lower the value of the dollar. Other things which supply dollars are U.S. tourists, U.S. military bases abroad, or U.S. companies building or buying factories overseas.

It is just the reverse for exports. Dollars come from abroad to fulfill the demand for American goods and services and increase the value of the dollar. Things which increase the dollar's value are U.S. exports, foreign tourists in the U.S., foreign companies setting up shop here, foreigners buying United States government bonds, real estate, or corporate stocks and bonds, and U.S. multinationals sending profits made overseas back home.

The other thing which will affect the value of the dollar is direct intervention by governments. If the Federal Reserve wants to affect the value of the dollar, it will just step into the market (secretly) and buy or sell (demand or supply) dollars.

Think of it. The dollar was being used by the majority of people around the globe who wanted to buy and sell on the world market. Other countries sold products, got dollars in return, and used those dollars to buy more products. The U.S. Treasury, on the other hand, needed only to crank up the printing press, separate the small bills from the large, and the country instantly had more purchasing power. Practically speaking, it means that the U.S. can go for long stretches buying more than it sells, because people are willing to hold dollars. Since 1982, the country has racked up a cumulative trade deficit of over $500 billion.

That was the benefit for the United States. But there was also a cost. To retain its role as world money, the dollar had to be kept high. Otherwise, investors would lose confidence. At first, a high dollar didn't matter much. The U.S. was consistently exporting more than it was importing, and this naturally kept the value of the dollar high. Job loss wasn't a problem because our productivity and competitive position were so much better than anyone else's.

During the 1950s and 1960s, the dollar was also kept high because its price was fixed. This collapsed in the early seventies when the values of currencies were allowed to vary with market forces. Immediately, the dollar began a ten-year decline. This was no surprise, since the dollar had been kept artificially high for so long. This decline, or depreciation, was good for U.S. manufacturers, who had already begun to experience competition from abroad.

But the boost to manufacturing came at the expense of confidence in the dollar. As the dollar depreciated, its status as world money began to be jeopardized. OPEC producers, who had always priced their oil in dollars, threatened to use other currencies unless the dollar was stabilized. Schemes for other forms of world money sprang up. The large American banks which specialized in international business were unhappy as the competition from German, Swiss, and Japanese banks mounted. Their lives had always been a little easier because their currency was world money.

By the summer of 1979, with U.S. inflation running at over ten percent, the foreign currency markets were getting jittery. Investors began to sell dollars. The dollar was slipping rapidly, and the international bankers wanted tough action.

The big banks demanded that the federal government halt the dollar's fall. Eventually President Carter was forced to fire his Chairman of the Federal Reserve, G. William Miller. In his place the bankers demanded one of themselves. David Rockefeller turned down the position and it went to Paul Volcker, New York international banker *par excellence.*

Volcker did his job. He raised interest rates, slapped on credit restrictions, and engineered what would eventually be a sixty percent rise in the value of the dollar. Banks who had been unhappy about the loss of the confidence in the dollar no longer had anything to fear. The United States and the world had entered a new phase, a period of worldwide "dollar shortage," which would keep the dollar high.[15] Economic policy was being shaped to satisfy the demands of big banks, who wanted a high dollar. The consequences for the trade deficit, unemployment, and social hardship were met with indifference.

How Workers Suffered from a High Dollar

The dollar was raised by an increase in interest rates, which led capital from around the world to flow stateside. This increased the value of the dollar because foreigners bought dollars. But almost immediately the high interest rates caused a recession, which reduced income and imports. The U.S. recession spread quickly to the rest of the world.

The rise of the dollar has had profound effects on American workers. It led us into the worst recession in postwar history. According to one estimate, the recession cost each American family $28,000.[16] And the high dollar itself has led to the loss of jobs. A recent study found that the rise of the dollar from 1981 to the beginning of 1985 can be held responsible for the loss of 1.3 million jobs in manufacturing.[17]

The dollar's rise has been seen by many as a policy mistake which can be easily remedied, perhaps by a new Chair of the Fed or a Democrat in the White House. This is naive. It is no accident that the dollar was substantially overvalued before 1971 and has been overvalued again through the 1980s. *The overvaluation of the dollar is a chronic or structural problem in the U.S. economy, caused by the dollar's role as world money.*

This may explain why Paul Volcker, even when faced with a record $170 billion trade deficit, opposed further depreciation.[18] Volcker did not want to see a repeat of the condition which put him into office in the first place—a lack of confidence in the dollar. And despite the hoopla about the recent fall of the dollar, it is

Who Cares About
The Value of the Dollar?

From one point of view, there's a great virtue to a high dollar: it means that U.S. goods fetch a high price on international markets. That makes imported consumer goods like VCRs, clothing, and wine cheaper; so consumers like a high value. Banks are another group which like a high dollar, especially banks whose business is primarily international. They benefit from the dollar's use as world money, and a high dollar keeps that role intact. A high dollar is also usually associated with low inflation, which banks like.

But a high dollar makes it harder for U.S. companies to sell abroad. So companies that export or companies whose products compete with imports like a low dollar.

For workers, a high dollar causes unemployment in industries involved in international trade. And even workers in other industries may be hurt by policies to keep the dollar high. The Federal Reserve Board often jacks up interest rates to trigger a recession, as it did in 1979. Increased interest rates lead capital to flow into the country, which raises the dollar.

still high. With a "correctly" valued dollar imports and exports would be equal.*

The effects of a high dollar may be put in historical perspective by a glance across the Atlantic. We may be repeating the fate of Britain, a country whose standard of living has fallen dramatically. For years the British government protected the pound sterling, which preceded the dollar as world money. It too was overvalued and eventually caused the decline of industry. The

---

* This is not meant to imply that the solution to today's trade deficit is further devaluation of the dollar. As anyone in business knows, goods can always be sold if the price is lowered enough. Rather than lower our standard of living by cheapening our currency, our trade imbalance could be corrected by a resumption of exports to Latin America, a reduction of military spending around the world, and productivity-enhancing investment.

government presided over this ruinous course because financial interests held a stranglehold over economic policy.

What's happening today to our manufacturing base shows the error in the high dollar strategy. The high dollar has reduced investment and productivity growth. High productivity growth is essential for a strong economy. And a strong economy is what produced confidence in the dollar in the first place. Restoring confidence by destroying the underlying strength of the economy is a strategy which is doomed to fail. People know this. That's why they're nervous about the trade deficit, the nation's status as the world's largest debtor, and the fragility of the economy.

Conclusion

We've covered a lot of ground. If we draw one lesson it is that the trade union movement should challenge Wall Street Internationalism. Once an economic boon, WSI is now at the core of the economic decline facing American workers. While unions have criticized free trade and capital mobility, opposition must go farther.

We have focused on three economic problems with WSI. First, corporations responded to foreign competition by moving offshore, leaving American workers with outmoded factories and fewer jobs. Second, the costs of squeezing the Third World are mounting, at home and abroad. U.S. workers are paying for the guns and ships which make it profitable for their employers to send their jobs overseas. Third, WSI is based on an overvalued dollar, which costs millions of jobs. Unless the world economy finds a new form of world money, we'll be stuck in an ever-tightening vise.

CHAPTER FIVE

Looking at Central America

There are lives in the balance.
There are people under fire.
Jackson Browne
"Lives in the Balance"

The U.S. government is at war in Central America. The fingers of that war directly touch Nicaragua, El Salvador, Honduras, and Guatemala, and reach out for Costa Rica, Panama, and Belize—twenty-seven million people in a region smaller than the state of Texas.

In Nicaragua, the United States has spent at least $250 million since 1980 on training, arming, and directing the contras in the battle to overthrow the Nicaraguan government. In El Salvador, the U.S. government has provided $1.5 billion to the fight against the rebel insurgency and stationed dozens of military advisors there. In Honduras, the Reagan administration has invested several hundred million dollars to build and staff a network of airports and military bases, causing great instability in the region's most impoverished country. In Guatemala, the United States recently restored military assistance to that nation's army despite its record as the worst violator of human rights in the Western Hemisphere.

In Costa Rica—a nation without armed forces—Washington has provided weapons and training to its police and urged the creation of a regular army. In Panama, the U.S. government continues to maintain a huge complex of military bases. Even in tiny Belize, the United States has begun a program of military training for the local defense force.

64

The annual cost of this presence is $9.5 billion.[1] In political terms, how is such a policy possible? Do the American people support the President and his policy in Central America?

The polls say no. Time after time, about two-thirds of those with an opinion are opposed to the American military buildup in Central America. Opposition is broad, but it is not deep. Soft public opinion does not translate into Congressional backbone.

Why Are We In Central America?

There have been few statements on why we are in Central America from the administration that are as honest and unintentionally revealing as President Reagan's first major anti-Nicaragua speech to the nation in April 1983:

> If Central America were to fall, what would be the consequences for our position in Asia and Europe and for our alliances such as NATO? If the United States cannot respond to a threat near our own borders, why should Europeans or Asians believe that we are seriously concerned about threats to them?... If we cannot defend ourselves there, we cannot expect to prevail elsewhere. Our credibility would collapse, our alliances would crumble and the safety of our homeland would be put in jeopardy.[2]

We assume that the President believes what he says. If so, the administration's policy towards Central America has little to do with democracy, or human rights, or freedom. It is not about improving the lives of Central American people. It has to do with maintaining a particular vision of America's role in the world.

The unspoken reasons for our government's obsession with Central America are much more convincing than the explanations usually offered.

○ Although Central America is not itself of great economic importance to multinational corporations and banks, the whole of Latin America and the Caribbean is. If nations in the hemisphere were to exercise greater control over their own resources, it could threaten multinational corporate power and the system of Wall Street Internationalism.

○ Central America operates as a symbol of the need to maintain high levels of military spending. That spending has been essential to the recovery of the Reagan years.

○ Central America is used to keep anticommunism alive as the rationale for the reassertion of U.S. power around the world.

Central America is not primarily valuable to the U.S. because of its economic worth, though there are of course corporations with large investments there. It has no important raw materials. It accounts for an insignificant portion of U.S. trade.

Latin America, however, is not small change. It is of tremendous economic and political interest to the U.S. government, military, banks, multinationals, insurance companies, and airlines.

Eighty percent of all U.S. investment in the Third World is in Latin America. Citibank makes nearly as much money in Brazil as it does in the United States. Latin America is second only to Western Europe as a market for U.S.-made goods. The U.S. and Mexico have a particularly intricate relationship, sharing the only important border in the world between an industrialized and an underdeveloped country. The debt owed by Latin nations to U.S. banks is larger than the Pentagon's budget.

Central America is scarcely in this picture. Nevertheless, it is a region of vital importance to the perception of "stability," and stability in the rest of the hemisphere is the prerequisite for protecting investments and getting debts paid. For U.S. government officials, unrest or instability *anywhere* in the hemisphere is cause for alarm.

In this scheme, the modest but profound efforts of the Nicaraguans in literacy, health, or land reform take on a menacing quality. The Nicaraguan revolution posed the threat of a good example and the contra war has temporarily derailed most of the promising changes. The desire of any Central American country to diversify its economic relations and reduce dependence on U.S. multinationals is viewed as disruptive of economic relations between North and South.

The second reason the administration promotes Central America as—in the words of former U.N. Ambassador Jeane Kirkpatrick—"the most important region in the world today" is that the crisis helps justify high levels of military spending in an era of domestic budget-cutting.

Indeed, military spending is the only ideologically acceptable form of deficit spending in American political culture today. This military Keynesianism is the Reagan administration's version of the public works projects of the thirties or CETA jobs in the seventies. The fact that military spending is an inefficient way to create jobs is rarely mentioned. Any serious challenge to increased military expenditures is discredited as soft on communism.

Finally, Central America is being used to reinvigorate the ideology of anticommunism. Viet Nam and detente reduced public support for superpower hostility. Americans understood that nationalism, not communism, was motivating change in the world. In 1976, President Jimmy Carter declared that the United States was no longer driven by an "inordinate fear of communism," and the public opinion polls bore him out.

Under President Reagan, anticommunism has staged an official comeback. It has been used to justify the growth in our military budget as well as intervention in the Third World. In Central America, poor people, nationalists, even the religious community have allied with marxists and radicals. The presence of marxists in these movements provides the right wing with ammunition for their holy crusade.

There is nothing new in today's policy. In 1927, Calvin Coolidge's Undersecretary of State, Robert Olds, explained why the Marines were fighting a war in Nicaragua against a guerrilla army led by the original Sandinista, Augusto Cesar Sandino.

> The Central American area...constitutes a legitimate sphere of influence for the United States, if we are to have due regard for our own safety and protection....Our ministers accredited to the five little republics...have been advisers whose advice has been accepted virtually as law...we do control the destinies of Central America and we do so for the simple reason that the national interest dictates such a course...

> [T]he Nicaraguan crisis is a direct challenge to the United States....Until now Central America has always understood that governments which we recognize and support stay in power, while those which we do not recognize and support fall. Nicaragua has become a test case. It is difficult to see how we can afford to be defeated.[3]

Fighting the Sandinistas, in the 1927 or 1987 incarnation, is important because, well, the administration says it is and then must back up its words. Language is corrupted, and terrorists are magically transformed into freedom-fighters.

Elliot Abrams, the present-day successor to Robert Olds, may appear weekly on *Nightline* to defend the administration's policies as justified attention to our "backyard." But the truth is that Nicaragua is nobody's backyard. Until U.S. policy reflects that fact, conflict in the region will continue.

It takes but a moment of putting yourself in their shoes to understand why this is so: no person—and no nation—wants to be an indentured servant to a great power. Central American nations were subservient to Spain, then to England, and for the last eighty years to the United States. We should not wonder that they consider the Monroe Doctrine to be more an example of superpower arrogance than a natural law protecting the hemisphere. President Reagan's remarkable statement that he wants to make Nicaragua "cry uncle" is the comment of a bully, not a statesman. The administration cannot look at Central America from a Central American point of view because to do so would give the lie to their entire policy.

The history books may show that the greatest mistake of the Sandinistas was coming to power at the wrong time in the wrong place. Whether a Democratic victory in the 1988 election will resolve the crisis depends on whether enough Democrats are willing to confront the soft-on-communism charge. This will depend on what labor and other constituency groups are saying.

In the interim, most of what our government does in Central America is far removed from the average American's daily life. Since 1980, only some seventy U.S. soldiers have died there, mostly in training accidents in Honduras—not a high enough number to sound the Congressional alarm. American policies are perhaps not so distant for the families of those seventy young soldiers. Nor, we suspect, are they for the millions of Central Americans who—if one can inject sentiment into the hard-headed world of politics for a moment—undoubtedly love their children no less than North Americans do.

Nicaraguan Labor—Pro and Contra

The rhetorical battle about Nicaragua is conducted at full volume. AIFLD's basic contention is that the Nicaraguan government represses the anti-Sandinista unions while unfairly promoting the pro-government federations. AIFLD's Doherty has charged that "the Sandinista dictatorship is even worse than the Somoza dictatorship,"[4] and once made the remarkable claim that the Sandinistas were comparable to the Nazis.[5] The pro-Sandinista unions are not viewed as legitimate representatives of the workers. Simply put, the Sandinista unions allegedly violate all of the basic standards by which the AFL-CIO evaluates other unions.

Labor's progressive wing responds to these charges in a variety of ways. The notion that life for unionists in Somoza's Nicaragua was better is dismissed as nonsensical: a passing knowledge of Nicaraguan history reveals that union activity was basically illegal for almost thirty years, save for company unions permitted to operate at a few Somoza-owned companies. A more substantial charge is that the pro-Sandinista unions are promoted while the rival unions are harassed and prevented from building their organizations. This is partly true, and troubles many left-leaning American unionists. But it is nevertheless necessary to point out that the Sandinistas enjoy great popular support, and that the Nicaraguan revolution was not exported from anywhere. Advances for farmworkers—the most important sector of organized labor—have solidified popular sentiment for the Sandinistas. Even with the hardship and discontent produced by the war, working-class support for the revolution is strong.

Are the pro-government Nicaraguan unions "transmission belts" of the state in the Stalinist sense? It's unlikely. There are vibrant disagreements inside the pro-revolutionary unions, with the angriest attacks on the Sandinistas coming from the left, not the right. Is the suspension of the right-to-strike a first step down the road to totalitarianism? Without a crystal ball it is impossible to answer this question, as events are still unfolding. But U.S. citizens might recognize in Nicaragua's actions the no-strike pledges made by U.S. unions during World War II. Whether the Nicaraguan prohibition on wartime strikes is similarly justified can be debated, but to call it Stalinist or totalitarian is a rush to judgment.

The situation for the main anti-Sandinista federation (the CUS) is a difficult one. Its failure to condemn contra terror against pro-Sandinista trade unionists causes great anger. It is linked to the contra cause by membership in a civilian opposition group called the Coordinadora, as well as by willingness to accept quasi-official U.S. aid. The Coordinadora is an employer-dominated group, which gives rise to the charge against the CUS that it is acting as a company union.

The jury is out on whether the CUS is weak and unpopular because of government harassment or because it is identified with Somoza (and the U.S.). The more important question is this: how would U.S. workers during World War II have responded to a union whose leadership was cold towards the war effort and warm towards the enemy. To ask the question is to answer it.

One final point must be made on the noisy question of union freedom, or the lack of it, in Nicaragua. The Sandinistas have acted harshly towards some opposition unionists. *Americas Watch* has documented arrests, detentions, and psychological pressures on union opponents that are violations of civil and trade union rights. But even AIFLD's leaders concede that not one labor opponent of the government has been killed, maimed, or disappeared.[6] This stands in contrast, vivid contrast, to the situation in El Salvador or Guatemala, where literally thousands of unionists have been killed, often mutilated, by death squads organized by the armies and governments of those countries. It is one thing to be harassed. It is another to be killed. The depiction of Nicaragua as some sort of giant torture house may serve as useful propaganda for the Reagan administration. It does not serve the cause of truth.

CHAPTER SIX

Toward A New Foreign Policy For Labor

*This is no time to be fighting each other
What we need, what we need—Solidarity.*
Steven Van Zandt
"Solidarity"

If the arguments of this essay are correct, labor will have to break with the assumptions that have steered it through the postwar era. This will take us into uncharted territory. Before offering our suggestions on a new foreign policy for labor, we consider the arguments for maintaining the present course.

"Free Trade Unionism" and the "Single Standard"

Since we have been critics of AFL-CIO international policies, it is prudent and fair to describe how the Department of International Affairs understands the principles that guide its foreign policy.

The yardstick that the DIA applies to determine its official posture toward a country is the degree to which "free trade unionism" exists. Those nations where it does exist are allies; those who repress or control unions are enemies.

There are three basic components to the judgment:

° The unions must be free of government control.

71

○ The unions must not be subordinated or subservient to a political party to the detriment of their own members.

○ Genuine freedom of association must be guaranteed. The right to organize, strike, and bargain collectively are contained within freedom of association.[1]

Using these principles, the Department of International Affairs has developed what it calls "a single standard on dictatorships." Opposition to governments of the left (U.S.S.R., Angola, Cuba, Chile before Pinochet), is matched by opposition to those of the right (South Africa, Paraguay, South Korea, Chile since Pinochet).

This single standard is what allegedly separates the AFL-CIO from conservatives in the State or Defense Departments. The federation says it upholds a higher standard of freedom and does not cave in and offer support to authoritarian, but pro-U.S. dictators. Conversely, they are skeptical of the leftist rhetoric of workers' rights and imperialism. They see Soviet expansionism as the force behind much popular discontent. A shorthand account might describe the DIA policy as combining anticommunism, labor rights, and national security.

Do these standards hold up? Are they applied with integrity? Should American unionists always accept the judgments of the Department of International Affairs?

We think not. The criteria for free trade unionism described above are fair enough, but the application is not. They have been too often distorted by anticommunist rigidity as well as inattention to local conditions and history. Even the briefest glance reveals all sorts of inconsistencies in the DIA's evaluation of trade unionism around the globe.

In Mexico, the union movement is so completely intertwined with the government bureaucracy and the ruling party as to be indistinguishable. Yet Mexican unions receive little of the hostility routinely aimed at the Nicaraguan unions for their ties to the government and ruling party.

Israel's giant HISTADRUT federation is intimately tied to the Labor Party and for years has had a *political* as opposed to a strictly trade union agenda. These ties are considered legitimate, whereas a major Salvadoran federation's political connections are leftist, and therefore illegitimate.

Our argument is not that the Mexicans or Israelis should be censured along with the others. In the Mexican or Israeli con-

Solidarity—East and West

Unfortunately, in the present climate of debate within the AFL-CIO, the criticisms that we have made will be dismissed as irresponsible or naive. We will be accused of harboring a hidden political agenda. Therefore, let us put our political views on the table.

Our criticism of the AFL-CIO's foreign policy should in no way be interpreted as support for the Soviet model of trade union policy or practice.

We reject the frozen conception of superpower politics that has infected and weakened the labor movement here, in the Soviet Union, and throughout the world. There are more choices than the two offered by the superpowers.

We have few illusions about Soviet-style unions. Workers in Eastern Europe lack the rights of association and organization that are the hallmarks of genuine trade unionism. The complex reality faced by workers there requires a new kind of trade union strategy. Transplanting the Western variety would be as inadequate as perpetuating the current state dominated model. The attempt to organize an independent grass roots union—Poland's Solidarity—highlights the failures of the existing organizations.

Solidarity's Gdansk demands—among the greatest union proposals ever—are as threatening to Communist rule as they would be to capitalist. In our view of the world, support for Polish workers and South African workers and, yes, even Nicaraguan workers is part and parcel of what trade union solidarity is all about.

text, those unions have made decisions in what they consider their own best interest.

An honest look at the record forces the acknowledgment that the DIA's real yardstick is the cold war. How a given country fits into the East-West framework will determine its standing. But it is a framework that is inadequate for dealing with local realities.

The single standard turns out to be anything but. There is one standard for pro-Soviet, non-aligned, or socialist countries and a second for pro-U.S. regimes. The latter, usually under the rule of a repressive leader, are not totally ignored, but the status of their unions and workers receives comparatively little attention from the DIA. Outrage is reserved for the first category.

The AFL-CIO's international program is characterized by more than cold war commitment. Secrecy is another distinguishing trait. Whether one is a supporter or critic of DIA actions, no rational observer can ignore the shield of bureaucratic expertise and self-righteousness that prevents open consideration of international issues. Some unionists argue that this secrecy is as disturbing as the ideological blinders constricting labor's foreign policy in the first place.

The unhappy result is that there is no room for debate. Mild questioning is taken for hostile fire. The questioner will be told that he or she is either a dupe or a sadly misinformed, if well-meaning colleague. The content of any criticism is ignored; instead, the critic's loyalties are challenged. The DIA retains sole power to decide who is and who is not a legitimate and free trade unionist.

Obviously, our account would be disputed by the leaders of labor's foreign institutes and the DIA. In theory, everything that any of the AFL-CIO institutes does overseas is accountable to the leadership, and hence the membership of the affiliates. In practice, the Department of International Affairs and the regional institutes (AIFLD, plus one each for Africa, Asia, and Europe) operate like a separate empire, accountable to almost no one in the labor movement.

The reasons for this are familiar to every labor leader, member, or staffer. Union officials—from shop steward to international president—rarely have the time or knowledge to follow, let alone challenge, the complex comings-and-goings on the international labor scene. Committed leaders and active members have more than enough to keep them occupied at home, especially in these days of union-busting and management take-aways. The DIA's policies and budget have been of minor concern to unionists who are busy servicing their membership or conducting organizing drives.

The structure of the AFL-CIO produces this situation: foreign affairs is the only important prerogative of the Washington-based central federation. The federation does not normally interfere in the internal activities of an affiliate. Similarly, the affiliate unions have traditionally steered clear of the "foreign desk;" most lack the resources to present an alternative. Long the exclusive preserve of national staff and leaders, the affiliate unions have been extremely reluctant—until recently—to trespass on that turf. The debate on Central America has reduced some of that reluctance.

The Terms of the Debate

When the Sunday morning talk shows come on, the interviewers put on their serious faces, pitch their voices low, and dive into the issue at hand by asking what they presume are tough, probing questions.

Unfortunately, they never ask the single most important question in any political or economic controversy: *what are the terms of the debate itself, and who set them?* If you have the power to frame the agenda and choose the language that gets used in any discussion, you can almost always shape the outcome.

Trade unionists know this fact of political life instinctively. They are more familiar with it than most Americans, if for no other reason than that they usually get the short end of the stick when it comes time to frame the issues. Consider one example:

"The question for union members is whether to lower their expectations and their wages in order to keep the company profitable and their jobs intact" could be reformulated as "The question for management is whether the company is willing to destroy the livelihoods of its workers and disrupt the life of the community simply to earn a higher profit in a lower-wage location."

That's the same question, really, but it reveals two different points of view. Management and the news media are more comfortable with the first question than the second, and so that is the way the issue is usually framed. Those workers and citizens who argue that labor rights and community needs should take precedence over the rights of private investment usually lose in the battle to set the agenda. The same holds true when the discussion turns to Central America or foreign policy. "Can the administration stop Soviet expansionism in Central America?" is one way to phrase it. "Can the American people understand that the unrest in Central America is the result of brutal conditions and U.S. hostility to reform?" is another.

The first formulation is preferred by the men and women who manage the news out of Washington. The second is the question that more and more trade unionists are asking.

What is really at stake in the labor movement's dispute on Central America is this power to frame the debate.

One of the most astute critics of the conservative position is Europe's Dan Gallin, secretary-general of the International Union of Food and Allied Workers. He writes that:

> The underlying ideology of the architects of AFL-CIO foreign policy...requires the defense of conservative interests and political values and has nothing to do, except in terms of propaganda for home consumption, with the defense of free and democratic trade unionism.

> There are, broadly speaking, two political perceptions today on what constitutes the major conflict in the world: according to one, the main conflict is the struggle between "East" and "West," and the main line of cleavage is the vertical one which divides the two superpowers and their zones of influence. The other perception is that the struggle that matters is between those below and those above, the exploited and their exploiters, the workers and their enemies, and this horizontal line of cleavage runs straight across both superpower blocs.

> The first perception is shared by conservatives in the West and the communist establishment in the U.S.S.R. and its dependencies. The second perception is the traditional one of the labour movement.[2]

It is to the second perception that we believe labor must return. We must get off the cold war merry-go-round. Ruthless adherence to the East-West blueprint is outdated and ill-serves workers in any country. The label of dedicated anticommunist that some veteran labor operatives have worn over the years is best left to the pathological nitwits in the basement of the White House.

Labor must also abandon its role as junior partner to business and government in the promotion of WSI. Free markets, free trade, and free flow of capital are the primary cause of the internationalizing of production that has led to runaway shops, decline of exports, floods of imports, and loss of organized labor's influence. It is a partnership without benefit.

There must be a new foreign policy for labor, arrived at through democratic debate. American workers are not experts, but that may not be such a disadvantage. The experts have as many failures as successes to their credit and could use the common sense that ordinary Americans bring to the foreign policy scene.

Finally, an atmosphere must be created within the labor movement in which workers feel that they can openly debate foreign policy questions without having their patriotism or loyalty questioned. Unions, for all their faults, are still among the most democratic institutions in American economic life, and can withstand a discussion of foreign affairs.

Principles of a New Foreign Policy for Labor

The specifics of a new foreign policy will emerge from debate inside unions. Even so, we offer some principles for that new policy.

°*A new foreign policy for labor must support free and democratic trade unions which allow workers in other nations the rights of self-determination and sovereignty that we hold dear for ourselves. They will not create copycat institutions: the context is different, the history is their own. Such pluralism is healthy.*

Freed from East-West tunnel vision, labor in this country can recognize that upheaval in the Third World is not directed or exported by anyone. Indeed, it may even be that a revolution is called for (South Africa comes to mind), as ossified or corrupt systems of power rarely reform themselves. Were U.S. unions to support their counterparts in Latin America in the battle for social change, it might be possible to reduce the violence of the struggle. At the least it would diminish the anti-U.S. feelings so common among Latin workers.

One does not expect the State Department to abandon its commitment to corporate America or pay more than lip-service to the rights of workers. But it is reasonable to hope that American unions will make a renewed effort at genuine internationalism.

°*A new foreign policy for labor must end the "shunning doctrine." The shunning doctrine is the AFL-CIO policy aimed at preventing contact with unions that do not have official federation approval. As it stands, affiliates are discouraged from communicating with unions deemed undesirable by the DIA.*

The only beneficiary of shunning is the multinational corporation that has workers scattered across the globe in unions of varying ideological beliefs. If French union workers are not invited to participate in an international conference of Ford workers because of their ties to French Communists, the real winner is the company. Contact with leftist unions need not imply an unabashed endorsement of their political positions. It simply recognizes that these workers face a common opponent.

In El Salvador, South Africa, and the Philippines, the shunning doctrine has meant that the largest and most important federations are ruled out-of-bounds by the gatekeepers at the DIA. This keeps the cold war flames hot, but it does not help U.S. trade unionists. Aid to the Third World should go to those unions who are accountable to their members and aggressive in fighting management, not to those who toe an American line.

° *A new foreign policy for labor must be tough-minded in its analysis of the Third World development strategy that calls for labor-management-government partnerships, a strategy known as tripartitism.*

The question of equitable economic development in Third World countries is a complicated one. Nevertheless, one simple fact has long been recognized by trade unionists—counting on the market to distribute the fruits of economic development does not work. Less powerful groups are cut out. Conscious effort and design is needed to spread the benefits around.

The chosen method is usually referred to as tripartite development. It involves cooperative ventures by government, business, and labor in an underdeveloped country. By joining hands in collective effort, everyone's stake in the success of a project is increased.

The tripartite model looks good on paper, but suffers from a bad case of wishful-thinking. It ignores power. It assumes that economic and political elites in a developing country will forego current gains for the uncertain promise of future ones. It is, in our opinion, a view that has been seriously undercut by recent experience.

In Asia, the tripartite "capitalist miracle" states of Taiwan, South Korea, or Hong Kong are not much more than miracles of repression. Unions are subject to intense legal restrictions and harassment is common. In Taiwan, some strike activity is punishable by death. The cost of the Asian miracle is freedom of association.

In Latin America, the situation is probably worse. Capital investment carrying any passport, local or U.S., has long had one objective: profit, as high and as quickly as possible, no matter the consequence. Heartfelt appeals for cooperation and a fairer sharing of wealth have fallen on especially deaf ears.

American unionists must recall that equity in the distribution of the economic pie depends not on government and business largesse or cooperation, but on union power and popular mobilization. The great legislative victories of organized labor—social security, unemployment insurance, fair labor standards, OSHA—like the great victories of the civil rights movement—the Voting Rights Act, affirmative action, Fair Housing—occurred because of ongoing, aggressive pressure on employers and the government, not because of congenial tripartite agreements.

°*A new foreign policy for labor must understand that anti-corporate or even pro-socialist sentiments among Third World workers are legitimate. There is an important democratic-socialist current in the worldwide labor movement, but the hard-liners of the DIA do not permit it an independent existence. For them, it is indistinguishable from the U.S.S.R.'s state communism.*

As Gallin noted, some American conservatives and Soviet authorities are closer to each other than they think: both sides fear an energized, activist popular movement, and so engage in complementary and equally narrow caricaturing of each other. Fortunately, working-class leaders throughout the rest of the world are not so hobbled by the East-West blinders. They are able to distinguish real socialism from the socialism of prisons, just as they understand that real freedom has little to do with freedom of the marketplace.

This independent, democratic-socialist current would be even more powerful if the American labor establishment reduced its hostility. The appeal of Soviet-style unionism may in part be due to American opposition to anything in between our version and theirs.

°*A new foreign policy for labor must take on the political task of monitoring and ultimately regulating the flow of capital around the world. Financial transactions now bear little relation to basic trade and commerce; they are caused by paper-shuffling, speculation, and profiteering.*

In early 1987, AFL-CIO secretary-treasurer Thomas Donahue gave a speech to the Japanese central labor federation on the link between economic growth and a healthy labor movement. Only growth, he argued, can reduce the tensions between competing groups of workers around the world.

Donahue is partly right, and partly wrong. By itself, growth will not solve our problems. Left to the market, growth will help some workers at the expense of others. Capital will still fly around the world leaving a wake of disruption. Growth is necessary, but it must be managed and environmentally sound if it is to empower workers around the world.

Controlling investment and capital flight is a critical first step for American unions. Decisions on where and how production takes place cannot be left solely to management. Labor must pose worker and community rights to the enshrined management rights clause in all union contracts.

It will take years for labor to come to grips with the enormous changes in the world economy. The first step is stating, loud and clear, that the right to make the decisions about how economic life will be structured does not belong to management alone. Exercising this right will involve more than seats on the Boards of Directors of large corporations. It will involve changing the legal and political environment in which the board decisions are made.

°*A new foreign policy for labor must unmask the competitiveness mania currently sweeping Congress and the nation's editorial pages.*

The bottom line of the competitiveness debate is lower wages. This is a game that workers can only lose. The way out of the competitiveness dead-end is, again, for labor to challenge the power traditionally reserved for management. Pleading for the best deal will not produce structural improvements or productivity gains, and the downhill slide of workers competing against each other will continue. The proposal by some steelworkers in Pennsylvania and Ohio for a worker-community-state "authority" on steel is a promising example of unionists who see themselves as producers, not merely employees. They have realized that solutions to deindustrialization and international competition must go beyond the traditional labor-management framework.

°*A new foreign policy for labor must get out of the trick bag of protectionism, which pits American workers against foreign workers.*

The important legislation aimed at protecting American jobs can do so only in the short run, but short term profitability for protected industries will not mean long term employment. Companies may diversify, automate, and invest profits in offshore production. There is no way to keep jobs without controls on capital investment and a trade policy that encourages decent working conditions and basic labor standards abroad.

°*A new foreign policy for labor must make common cause with labor's natural allies. By natural allies we mean those who share labor's interest in equitable economic and social relations and who believe that the infection of greed in today's world should be attacked, not applauded.*

Blacks, Latins, women, environmentalists, peace and religious activists, community organizers, gays, housing activists, senior citizens, the disabled, intellectuals, and many "single-issue" constituencies have a natural inclination to align themselves with unions and workers. But the obsession with "radicalism" abroad makes it hard for some labor leaders to join with "radicals" at home. It is important to remember that the main enemy is still corporate power, not other social movements.

°*A new foreign policy for labor must grow from discussion at all levels of the labor movement, from stewards' meetings to executive boards.*

The October 1987 AFL-CIO convention, only a few weeks away as we write, may or may not witness another full-scale debate on Central America, but no matter what happens there the genie is out of the bottle. The right and responsibility of trade unionists to consider problems of international economics and politics is now fully established. Efforts by conservatives to channel discussion onto the safer ground of bread and butter domestic issues is a diversionary smokescreen.

This is all to the good. A new way of thinking about the world—which is what a foreign policy is for, after all—is one of the crucial pieces in the jigsaw puzzle of a powerful labor movement. The dilemma facing labor is a serious one: will it permanently accept the junior partner role in society and the Democratic Party, or will it once again lead the way to a more equitable and just society? There is a real danger that organized labor could come to resemble little more than another pressure group if it fails to respond creatively to global economic and political pressures.

A world with dignity, respect, and a decent standard of living for common people everywhere simply cannot be established when our vision is restricted by a tired, cold war outlook. It's time we came out of the tunnel.

NOTES

Chapter One

1. Paula Voos, *Labor Union Organizing Programs 1954-1977*, Ph.D. Dissertation, Harvard University, May 1982.

2. William Serrin, "Industries, in Shift, Aren't Letting Strikes Stop Them," *New York Times*, September 30, 1986.

3. Economic Policy Institute, Briefing Paper, "Family Incomes in Trouble," (Washington: Economic Policy Institute), 1986, p. 26.

4. Ward Morehouse and David Dembo, "Joblessness and the Pauperization of Work In America," Background Paper (New York: Council on International and Public Affairs), May 1987.

5. Barry Bluestone and Bennett Harrison, "The Great American Jobs Machine," Paper Prepared for Joint Economic Committee, U.S. Congress, 1986, p. 17.

6. Lou Harris, "Americans and the Arts," Lou Harris poll, October 1984.

7. Lucy Gorham, "No Longer Leading," (Washington: Economic Policy Institute), 1986.

8. AFL-CIO Report #10, "Trade Job Loss: 2.5 Million," December 1986.

9. Democratic Staff of Joint Economic Committee, "Trade Deficits, Foreign Debt, and Sagging Growth," September 1986.

10. Authors' estimates. See chapter four.

11. For an account of Ford's attitudes see Robert Lacey's *Ford, The Men and the Machine*, (Boston: Little, Brown and Co.), 1986.

Chapter Two

1. Despite the postwar rhetoric of international egalitarianism, the United States ran the show. The poor countries, as well as the rich ones, had little say. Only Britain had any measure of influence.

2. See Thomas Ferguson, "From Normalcy to New Deal: Industrial Structure, Party Competition and American Public Policy in the Great Depression," *Industrial Organization*, Winter 1984, and Myra Wilkins, *The Maturing of Multinational Enterprise*, (Cambridge, Mass.: Harvard University Press), 1974.

3. See Wilkins, *op. cit.*

4. This estimate is from Fred Block, *The Origins of International Economic Disorder*, (Berkeley: University of California Press), 1977, p. 33.

5. The war and its aftermath provided the opportunity for American business to gain advantage vis-à-vis the Europeans, especially the British. We have mentioned the monumental struggle for Mideast oil. There was a more general scramble as well, involving diplomatic and indeed military means. A classic attitude was that of Nelson Rockefeller, who coordinated the government's office of Inter-American Affairs during the war. His office recommended that as collateral for wartime aid, the British be asked to put up their holdings in Chile and Argentina, "good properties in the British portfolio we might as well pick up now." The Rockefeller family, of course, had longstanding business interests in Latin America, and still does. (Memo cited in Peter Collier and David Horowitz, *The Rockefellers: An American Dynasty*, (New York: Holt, Rinehart, and Winston), 1976, p. 230.)

6. See Gar Alperovitz, *Atomic Diplomacy: Hiroshima and Potsdam—the Use of the Atomic Bomb and the American Confrontation with Soviet Power*, (New York: Viking Penguin), 1985.

7. Barry Blechman and Stephen Kaplan, *Force Without War*, (Washington: Brookings Institution), 1978.

Chapter Three

1. Radosh, *op. cit.*, p. 391.

2. *Ibid.*, p. 389.

3. Reuther, *op. cit.*, p. 420.

4. In 1980, the corporate seats on the board were eliminated, and AIFLD is now entirely union-run.

5. Reuther, *op. cit.*, p. 419.

6. Kwitny, *op.cit.*, p. 351-2.

7. Radosh, *op.cit.*, p. 423.

8. Reuther, *op. cit.*, p. 417.

Chapter Four

1. Felix Rohaytn, *The Twenty-Year Century*, (New York: Random House), 1980.

2. The U.S. share of world exports (excluding the centrally planned economies) dropped from 20% to 13.6% between 1951 and 1973. Japan increased from 2% to 7%, West Germany from 4.6% to 13%, and the European Economic Community as a whole from 27.6% to 40.6%. The Less Developed Countries fell from 33% to 23.5%. Source: *International Trade Statistics*, International Monetary Fund, various years.

3. This estimate was created by taking the annual job loss calculated over the periods 1966-72 and 1977-82. We assumed that job loss be-

tween 1973-76 was the average of the two periods, and that job loss after 1982 equalled the 1977-82 rate. The studies we used are Robert Frank and Richard Freeman, *Distributional Consequences of Direct Foreign Investment*, (New York: Academic Press), 1978; and Norman Glickman, Jose Casco-Flores and Geoffrey Bannister, "The Regional Impact of Overseas Investment by U.S. Multinationals," University of Texas at Austin, 1986.

4. Estimate from Peggy Musgrave, *Direct Investment Abroad and the Multinationals: Effects on the United States Economy*. (U.S. Senate, Committee on Foreign Relations, Subcommittee on Multinational Corporations, Committee Print, Ninety-Fourth Congress, first session), 1975. Musgrave's estimate is a 4% loss of labor income. The $900 figure is obtained by taking 4% of compensation of employees, then dividing by the number of employed persons. All data are for 1986, from the *Economic Report of the President*.

5. Gary Hufbauer and Jeffrey Schott, "The Soviet-European Gas Pipeline: A Case of Failed Sanctions," in Theodore Moran, *Multinational Corporations*, (Lexington, Mass.: D.C. Heath and Co.), 1985, pp. 227, 238.

6. Fred Halliday, *The Making of the Second Cold War*, (London: Verso Editions), 1983.

7. Charles Lipson, *Standing Guard: Protecting Foreign Capital in the Nineteenth and Twentieth Centuries*, (Berkeley: University of California Press), 1985, p. 98.

8. *Ibid.*, p. 103.

9. The growth rates for Latin America are lower (1.5%), and manufacturing exports from Africa are negligible. Data are from Ajit Singh and Alan Hughes, "The World Economic Slowdown and the Asian and Latin American Economies," paper presented at Conference on Global Macroeconomic Policies, World Institute for Development Economics Research, Helsinki, Finland, August 1986.

10. *World Development Report*, World Bank, 1985, p. 40.

11. *Ibid.*, p. 32.

12. Joint Economic Committee of the U.S. Congress, "The Impact of the Latin American Debt Crisis on the U.S. Economy," Staff Study, May 1986.

13. Lance Taylor, "Economic Openness—Problems to the Century's End," paper presented at Conference on Global Macroeconomic Policies, World Institute for Development Economics Research, Helsinki, Finland, August 1986, p. 56.

14. Jobs With Peace, Campaign Report, v.1, #5, Winter 1987.

15. Gerald Epstein, "The Triple Debt Crisis," *World Policy Journal*, v.2, #3, 1985.

16. *Economic Report of the People*, Center for Popular Economics, (Boston: South End Press), 1986.

17. William Branson and James Love, "Dollar Appreciation and Manufacturing Employment and Output," National Bureau of Economic Research Working Paper #1972, 1986.

18. Volcker's September 24, 1986 testimony to Congress, printed in *Federal Reserve Bulletin*, November 1986, pp. 773-779.

Chapter Five

1. Cohen and Rogers, *Inequity and Intervention: The Federal Budget and Central America*, (Boston: South End Press), 1986.

2. *New York Times*, April 28, 1983.

3. Tom Barry and Deb Preusch, *The Central America Fact Book*, (New York: Grove Press), 1986, p. 3.

4. *Washington Times*, December 16, 1985.

5. Speech at international affairs seminar, AFL-CIO Convention, October 1985.

6. Samuel Haddad, AIFLD Assistant Executive Director, Speech to the Labor Press Council of Metropolitan New York, May 17, 1986.

Chapter Six

1. Michael Kerper, "The International Ideology of U.S. Labor, 1941-1975," University of Gothenberg, 1976.

2. News Bulletin, International Union of Food and Allied Workers' Associations, 1987, #1-2.

CENTRAL AMERICA COMMITTEES IN THE U.S. LABOR MOVEMENT

National Labor Committee
in Support of Democracy and
Human Rights in El Salvador
c/o ACTWU
15 Union Square West
New York, NY 10003

New York City
c/o Headwear Joint Board
99 University Place
New York, NY 10003

Washington, D.C.
c/o AFSCME
1625 L Street, NW
Washington, DC 20036

New Jersey
c/o CWA
10 Rutgers Place
Trenton, NJ 08618

Philadelphia
P. O. Box 7842
Philadelphia, PA 19101

Chicago
c/o Chicago Joint Board
ACTWU
407 So. Dearborn Street
Chicago, IL 60605

San Diego
P. O. Box 5431
San Diego, CA 92105-0080

Portland
P. O. Box 6443
Portland, OR 97228

Massachusetts
104 Auburn Street
Cambridge, MA 02139

Michigan
c/o AFSCME Local 1640
11000 W. McNichols, #B-7
Detroit, MI 48221

Atlanta
P. O. Box 1282
Atlanta, GA 30301

San Francisco
255 Ninth Street
San Francisco, CA 94103

Oakland
P.O Box 28014
Oakland, CA 94604

Delaware
407 W. 21st Street
Wilmington, DE 19802

Seattle
P.O. Box 28090
Seattle, WA 98119

PACCA BOOKS

INEQUITY AND INTERVENTION

The Federal Budget and Central America
Joshua Cohen and Joel Rogers
A Domestic Roots book
Cohen and Rogers provide a useful discussion of the recent history of the Federal Budget and the fiscal policies of the Reagan administration, and focus on the costs of maintaining a capacity to intervene in the third world and the domestic implications.

South End Press, $4.75

RULES OF THE GAME

American Politics and the Central America Movement
Joshua Cohen and Joel Rogers
A Domestic Roots Book
Why is political action so difficult in the United States, and why are there "striking gaps between public opinion and public policy" in this country? The authors provide a mini-textbook on American politics geared to the needs of activists.

South End Press, $4.75

FORGING PEACE

The Challenge of Central America
Richard Fagen
Explaining the crucial link between peace and development in Central America, *Forging Peace* explains the reasons for the failure of current U.S. policy toward the region and puts forward a comprehensive alternative.

Basil Blackwell, $7.95

TRANSITION AND DEVELOPMENT

Problems of Third World Socialism
Richard Fagen, Carmen Diana Deere, and Jose Luis Coraggio, editors
A critical examination of the problems that third world countries encounter when they try to make a transition to socialism.

Monthly Review Press, $12.00